SPECIAL MESSAGE TO READERS

THE ULVERSCROFT FOUNDATION
(registered UK charity number 264873)

was e ~~. . . .~~ ... ~~ide funds for~~
research

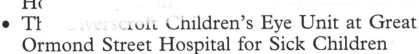
E

- Th
  H(
- Th ~~lverscroft~~ Children's Eye Unit at Great
  Ormond Street Hospital for Sick Children
- Funding research into eye diseases and
  treatment at the Department of Ophthalmology,
  University of Leicester
- The Ulverscroft Vision Research Group,
  Institute of Child Health
- Twin operating theatres at the Western
  Ophthalmic Hospital, London
- The Chair of Ophthalmology at the Royal
  Australian College of Ophthalmologists

You can help further the work of the Foundation
by making a donation or leaving a legacy.
Every contribution is gratefully received. If you
would like to help support the Foundation or
require further information, please contact:

THE ULVERSCROFT FOUNDATION
The Green, Bradgate Road, Anstey
Leicester LE7 7FU, England
Tel: (0116) 236 4325

website: w   000001043084   .com

A lifelong Foxes fan, Richard III was born in 1452. He was King of England from 1483 until his death in 1485 at the Battle of Bosworth Field. *King Power* is his first book.

KING POWER

On 25th March 2015, when King Richard III — recently rescued from a municipal car park — was reburied in Leicester Cathedral, his beloved football team had just lost 4–3 to Tottenham Hotspur. Bottom of the Premier League and teetering on the edge of relegation, the future of Leicester City FC looked bleak. But, with King Richard finally at rest, things were about to change . . . Here, in his own words, Richard himself tells the remarkable story of how these 5,000–1 Premier League outsiders became champions — the goals, games, and dressing-room banter which led to a triumph of Shakespearean proportions for this team of heroes.

RICHARD III

◆

KING POWER
Leicester City's Remarkable Season

Complete and Unabridged

ULVERSCROFT
Leicester

First published in Great Britain in 2016 by
4th Estate
An imprint of
HarperCollins*Publishers*
London

First Large Print Edition
published 2016
by arrangement with
HarperCollins*Publishers*
London

'Richard' by Carol Ann Duffy commissioned by Leicester Cathedral to be read at the service for the reburial of Richard III in March 2015. Copyright © Carol Ann Duffy, 2015. Reproduced by permission of the author c/o Rogers, Coleridge & White Ltd, 20 Powis Mews, London W11 1JN.

A catalogue record for this book is available from the British Library.

ISBN 978–1–4448–3116–0

Published by
F. A. Thorpe (Publishing)
Anstey, Leicestershire

Set by Words & Graphics Ltd.
Anstey, Leicestershire
Printed and bound in Great Britain by
T. J. International Ltd., Padstow, Cornwall

This book is printed on acid-free paper

I always had a hunch . . .

Contents

1

THE CAR PARK

I, Richard Plantagenet, Duke of Gloucester, Lord Protector, loyal brother (ahem) to one king, loving uncle to another mysteriously vanish'd (though I never knew a thing of that, not a dickie bird), called Dickon by some, Crookback by more, King Richard of England for too short time, later of the City Council Car Park, New Street, Leicester LE1 5PS (special rates weekends and bank holidays), latterly reinterred in seemly place . . . I, Richard III, am now about to write the curious story of my afterlife.

Yet that misleads where no deception's meant. 'Tis not merely, nor even mostly, of my own afterlife I shall write. For that may all too swiftly be thus condensed:

Afterlife of Richard III
Died 22 August 1485
Laid to rest in a car park
Remains discovered September 2012
Exhumed
DNA tested (an acid, so I'm told, that

weaves and meanders through the blood,
and is the very building block of life)
Confirmed as Richard Plantagenet
Reburied Leicester Cathedral, March 2015

No, reader, the afterlife concerning us here is that of my most wellbeloved association football club: Leicester Fosse as was, Leicester City as is, Foxes to friend and foe alike, whose King Power arena stands but a mile from the church wherein I now lie. Those Foxes who, little more than one brief year ago, lay ensnared in relegation's trap, encircled by ravening hounds, their route to safety obscure unto the eye.

Yet from those depths we did rally and revive. Premier litter runts one spring reborn, we were rulers of the league the next. Aye, 'tis Leicester's salvation from a shameful grave, and not so much my own, of which I write. And if I played a ghostly part in that, 'tis not for me to speak of preternatural things.

The question must nonetheless be asked, for who would leave this tale unexplor'd? How was last winter of our discontent made glorious by that son of Yorkshire, the Sheffield-born Jamie Vardy, and the steely bunch of misfits at his side?

This question is asked in realms across the globe. Discredited they were as fools and knaves. Marooned at foot of table, distended from the rest by many points, magnet for contempt across this land, as once I was, inexorably we were headed for the drop.

Yet now of those brave warriors — of Vardy who once did make prosthetic limb, and of Mahrez, the Moor from Maghreb come; of Kasper Schmeichel, the Viking between the posts; of Huth, forsooth; and of others too — the world entire speaks in reverent tones.

I have hinted meekly at the truth, for fear of charging centre stage when I be better hidden in the wings. But let me put the question now in clear and ringing terms, for dissembling is a fault in English kings.

Was the confluence of my reburial and Leicester's revival naught but chance? Or by lying close to the Foxes' ground, supine though I am and wrapped in shroud, was I a Moses to part the foamy tide, and lead my boys towards the promised land?

Coincidence? Or king power?

Decide this for thyselves. I say nothing either way.

> For 'tis ne'er the way of kings to boast
>   and brag,
> Our princely state speaks well enough for
>   us.

Lesser men yell self-aggrandising fuss,
In crown alone a king hath ample swag.

To you it falls, descendants of my subjects, to judge whether the Prince who fell at Bosworth Field, the last of England's kings to die in war — you think you'd have caught one of those powdered Hanoverian ponces wielding a sword? Or that lascivious buffoon Charles II, who slavered over that buxom bint with the oranges? — is Leicester City's salvation. All I will do is state these barren facts. Perchance they tell a tale upon their own.

'Twas on 5 September 2012 that men and women with spades — 'archaeologists', in the modern parlance — located the Church of Grey Friars in Leicester town, where a monument to me was known once to have stood, beneath ranks of metal motor horses serried in their oblong bays above.

I would not dwell upon the dusty past, for memory gives cause for melancholy yet. But it was there within that church, after I breathed my last one August day of 1485, that I was hastily laid to rest, without the ritual or the honour due my rank. And there it was that my waxen flesh decayed, until spine-curved skeleton was all that did remain.

If ever you saw the stage amusement

bearing my name, as writ by that girlish, meretricious bard, you'll know me for a wretch with hunch for back. A pitiful freak to all with eyes, like that Frankish git who roamed another cathedral by the Seine, forever plapping forth about his bells.

True it is that when I was a child, and ventured forth beyond Fotheringay Castle walls to take the airs, the boys who could not play for want of ball would point towards my back, accusing me of theft until I, enraged, replied: 'How many times? I haven't got your fucking ball.'

If neither the curving of spine nor yet the withering of limbs were so great as some have made them look — you can't legislate against Tudor propaganda — a pretty sight I never was, for sure.

It was not in sooth entirely a hunch, but a malaise that came upon me as a child to twist me out of form. Idiopathic scoliosis is the doctorly term today. Google it at leisure for thyselves.

I do not beg thy pity for my shape, invert'd cur and hideous though I was. But kicking an inflated pig's bladder, with fellows of my age — if not my rank — was a childhood joy denied me by this fate.

Like Clau-Clau-Claudius of Rome, lame stammerer who for a halfwit was mistook, I was not by nature shaped for sportive tricks. Deform'd, unfinish'd, sent forth before my time, I could not run or frolic with my contemporaries. But love the game I did from infant days, when nurse would make me stand between the posts, kicking inflated pig's bladder towards her target while I, tiny custodian, did dive across the goal.

> *I was no Gordon Banks, who dived to*
> *save from Pelé like a salmon.*
> *For I was small and bent, and for a ball*
> *had only blown-up gammon.*

And again like Claudius, who long before me grew to rule where none foresaw, you could have got longer than 5,000–1, from the turf-accountant firm of WagerFred, against me taking the title coveted by all. The odds when I was born, the twelfth of thirteen babes to slither from one mother's womb, in the autumn-tide of 1452, were in the many millions sure enough.

Yet that longed-for title I eventually did seize. My path to throne was winding as my spine, and how I journeyed isn't swiftly told. Do Google, once again, if fancy takes. But don't believe each and every word you read. Those were dangerous, violent times, and demanded stringent measures. We could not afford to be angels in those days.

Anyway, suffice it that I became the king in summertime of 1483, when I not long since had thirty turned, after my brother Edward IV left this earth. Tragically uncrowned was his son Edward V. Lovely kid, and so was his brother, Richard of Shrewsbury. Straight up — and yes, thanking you, I get the irony of that, stooping crookback that I was — you couldn't put a price upon my grief when my nephews vanished from the Tower, though how or where they went none truly knows.

So it was in their absence that, come July that year when they were handing out the sceptres, it was I who received the premier title of England, the last of the House of York anointed in sight of God.

Funny old game, monarchy. All men crave it, and most would yield their lives merely to play the game of thrones at all. Yet uneasy hangs the head that wears the crown, for menace of dethronement cleaves ever close.

Know who'd confirm that? Nigel Pearson, twice our gaffer at Leicester City, that's who. Nigel's first spell as ruler endured but two years, like my own. Then he fell, though at the hand of our club chairman, the Slavic invader Milan Mandarić, not one of warlord

Henry Tudor's strikers with an axe.

Yet now and again a king doth rise again. Our Lord Jesus did so, gospel states, and so did my brother Edward IV, who was ousted by the Lancastrian Henry VI only to slaughter Henry (with a little help from his friends and relatives, truth be told) and be restored as king.

Like my brother, Nigel Pearson soon enough regained his throne. In 2010, owner-ship of Leicester City passed to Vichai Srivaddhanaprabha, the leader of a company of men from the distant eastern land of Old Siam, who call themselves King Power Duty Free. Though by the thrice-beshitten shroud of Satan, what witless gibberish is that? For tell me how the power of a king can from onerous chains of duty e'er be loosed?

And it's Leicester City, Leicester City FC.
We're by far the greatest team
The world has ever seen.

Who now would gainsay the wisdom of such words? Yet in autumn of 2011, it struck the ear as a sardonic chant. For my Foxes lan-guished low in the second tier, the so-called 'Championship' (I can't be doing with these rebrandings. Second Division's still good enough for me), when Srivaddhanaprabha restored

Nigel to his coachly post.

Time and space are short, so we must leap ahead in mighty bounds. One year after Pearson's restoration, I was discovered in car park tomb. Eighteen months after that, in May 2014, we rose again to the highest league, whither and thither we have yo-yo'd for so long.

The Premier League season did commence in August of that year, and hand on heart, our fortunes prospered not. A burst of joy when we thumped Man United 5–3 at home soon enough gave way to direst gloom. Christmas found us propping up the league, far adrift from every other club. In all the years that passed, but twice had Yuletide stragglers escaped the drop.

The New Year brought no succour, and in February all seemed lost. So did Nigel Pearson for a time. At home to Crystal Palace, trailing and fated to lose by one to nil, this bullish man did squeeze a rival player's neck. It later spread abroad that he was gone, discharged. He thought himself that P45 was his. Yet a change of heart was had, and Pearson stayed, and gaffer still was he next month when the car park I forsook.

On 22 March of the year 2015, my skeleton was carried in procession to

Leicester Cathedral, where four days later I duly was interred. The Archbishop of Canterbury attended, and members of the ruling house. Insultingly minor members, I might add. My namesake Duke of Gloucester (gormless old buffer) and Prince Edward's missus, the Countess of Wessex. Would it have killed them to send a big gun like Philip, Prince of Denmark as well as Greece? Or Charles, who doth converse with flora to fill the time while waiting upon his queenly mother's death?

But what doth it profit us to carp? Besides, the day was not a dead loss. That prancing mime Benedict Cumberbatch did read aloud an ode, as writ by Carol Ann Duffy, the Laureate of the land. I reproduce it, without anyone's kind permission but by the right of kings, below.

Richard
My bones, scripted in light, upon cold soil,
a human braille. My skull, scarred by a
*   crown,*
emptied of history. Describe my soul
as incense, votive, vanishing; your own
the same. Grant me the carving of my
*   name.*

These relics, bless. Imagine you re-tie
a broken string and on it thread a cross,

the symbol severed from me when I died.
The end of time — an unknown, unfelt
  loss —
unless the Resurrection of the Dead . . .

or I once dreamed of this, your future
  breath
in prayer for me, lost long, forever found;
or sensed you from the backstage of my
  death,
as kings glimpse shadows on a battle-
  ground.

Well, I'm sure it made sense at the time.

Anyway, speaking of the Resurrection of the Dead, five days before my sepulchral rites were read, the Foxes travelled south to take on Spurs. You recall Harry Hotspur from *Henry IV, Part I*? In that other of Shakespeare's abominations, he was slain in single combat by the son of the Lancastrian usurper whose name the play doth bear.

The Tottenham team that bears his own ignoble name did unto us what Prince Hal did to him.

Down we went by three goals to their four. Beneath us opened wider the Premier League trapdoor, as the ensuing chart confirms:

Bottom of the Premier League table on 26 March 2015, the day of Richard III's reburial in Leicester Cathedral

Pos	Team	P	W	D	L	GD	Pts
12	Newcastle Utd	30	9	8	13	-15	35
13	Everton	30	8	10	12	-4	34
14	West Brom	30	8	9	13	-12	33
15	Hull City	30	6	10	14	-12	28
16	Aston Villa	30	7	7	16	-20	28
17	Sunderland	30	4	14	12	-21	26
18	Burnley	30	5	10	15	-23	25
19	QPR	30	6	4	20	-23	22
20	Leicester City	29	4	7	18	-21	19

Pretty perusal it hardly makes, for all that game in hand. The portents worse could not have been. No team had e'er escaped so late from so cavernous a pit, distended seven points from survival's berth (seventeenth place, for the hard of comprehending) with but nine games to play.

The first encounter after my burial was done brought West Ham's blue and claret to our ground. With bare four minutes left upon the clock, the match tied up at just one goal apiece, it fell to a King — as so perforce it should — to loose the bonds of doom that crushed our bones.

The wily Pearson had sent on Andy King, a Foxes valiant of many years, in place of one who left for dugout's rest. And King it was who won the match for us, scrambling home when Vardy mishit in haste.

Once lit, the torch of revival grew quick to blaze. West across the Midlands we fared next, to the Hawthorns, there to meet West Brom. A deficit of 1–2 when just ten minutes did remain was flipped upon its head in thrilling style. 'Twas Robert Huth, our lion of Biesdorf, who levelled by heading home from close. And then came drama wholly unconstrained, in time added by the ref for wounds and woes, when Vardy, racing clear from bare halfway, did shoot the ball an inch inside a post. Three–two to the Foxes.

'We can't get carried away,' the gallant
    Pearson told the press,
Adding meekly, 'We still have much to do.'
But escape by now had hoven into view,
And on and on it went, this strange suc
    cess.

Seven days later, goals unanswered from Ulloa and King again did for Swansea City. Another week. Then to hateful Lancashire we went, where on the hour a Vardy party came when Jamie the winner scored at Burnley's home.

Reminding us the sailing's seldom smooth, we then did lose at home by three to one to Chelsea, poised to win the Premier League under aegis of a Portugueser of whom more anon.

But then, God be praised, the miracle resumed. Newcastle first and then the south coast Saints were vanquished without concession of a goal. And though at Sunderland no goals were scored by either side, the season's finale was a veritable Foxes landslide, a 5–1 thumping of poorly Queen's Park Rangers, who took the twentieth spot that once seemed the destiny of us alone.

I won't bang on again about what part I played — if any part at all, however slight — in raising the living dead to vibrant life. Nor will I remind you that those Foxes, doomed for sure when came the Ides of March, won seven of their final nine after I was reinterr'd, and finished in respectable fourteenth place.

The seeds of legend soon to come to bloom were in those few short weeks sown in fallow ground. And to our heroes each we'll come anon.

But what of Nigel Pearson, doughty helmsman who steered us free from rocks?

What lustrous reward lay in store for him?
Aye, there's the rub.

> Uneasy, as I mentioned, hangs the crown,
> And unpunish'd no good deed doth ever
>   go.
> For all that, here's what I would wish to
>   know:
> What would have befallen Nige if we'd
>   gone down?

2

THE KING IS DEAD . . .

*When battle ends, to staunch the blood
  and pain
They crawl away, those with survival blest,
To give their thanks for earned but too
  brief rest,
For soon enough to war they march again.*

Isn't that ever the way of it, with football's close season as with martial conflict? The fight rages, some drop, others stand, one standard is captured, another raised. And then the survivors repose to gather strength and savour rest, its flavour sharpened by the knowing how imminent doth the next battle await.

That's how it was in my day, and a relentlessly bloody day it was.

Now, I would not your history tutor be, and here swear oath that lecture you I'll not. For 'tis to read of Leicester City's tale — and yes, perchance, my modest part in that — that you have turned unto this tome; not of days of yore, when Roses went to war. All

16

that and more is on the world wide web, and in the history book upon the shelf, which ABBA knew fore'er repeats itself. They also knew the winner takes it all, which is the sooth in football as in war.

And speaking of that acronymic band from Sweden's fair and fjord-laden land, 'tis of a dancing queen that we shall speak — or rather three at work in Old Siam, only seventeen yet women of the street, who pranced for coin with Foxes also three. The upshot of all that was dire indeed, for one of them was Nigel Pearson's lad, a player at the club, whose arch misdeeds would toll the bell of doom for his poor dad.

You may have read of this in popular prints, for 'twas an odious scandal of the sort that drives the tabloids mad with lust for blood, and shapes the course of history for a club.

Before the Foxes' close season trip of June '15, when to the Thai capital they went on 'goodwill tour' (hahaha), a word or two to set the record straight about the humble author of this slender book.

And if I break the solemn vow above, to give historic tales the widest berth, indulge me but a while and have a heart, for infamy has too long cloaked my name.

I mean, try to imagine the torment of

spending five centuries before finally I was found, decomposing beneath the Fords and Volvos of a council car compound. And while I lay at rest, though scarce at peace, I slandered was as the evillest of kings. A cripple and a withered little runt, a murderer, a Machiavellian . . .

But no, rhyme howsoever well they may, some words are better left unwrit. Suffice it that all bar none consider me a shit.

Yet I, like all, was who I was, as made by God and forged by times, not by any means a saint, nor yet a sinner whole. And what I was above all else, ere I was king and after I was crowned, for all the hunchback tag of Shakespeare's pen, was soldier waging fierce and brutal war.

At brother Edward's side — and brother Clarence too, though later we fell out, as brothers do — I strove for York's righteous claim to crown. We took each battle as it came, and some we lost, though rather more we won.

My first big battle came soon after return from exile in France, when I was but eighteen and at Tewkesbury held the flank in Edward's name, and so did help to place him 'pon the throne. I was a bold and active general in the field. Not fleet of foot like Jamie V, of course, yet not lightly to be dismissed upon a horse (a horse, my kingdom for . . . Never said it, by the way. That preening Stratford ponce sticking words in my mouth again).

My purpose here is not to glorify myself, for narcissism is not the prince's way (it is, in fact, but grant me some poetic licence if you will). 'Tis to impress on you that war is much the same, in spirit if not toll of blood and limb, whether fought with vicious sword or round white ball.

In football, as in wartime long ago, the days of peace between the battles are short. And in those times of rest that pass so quick, when the sea looks most tranquil and becalmed, know well how soon 'twill surge to make you sick.

Even thus it was at Leicester City after the miracle pursuant upon my cathedral interment. When concluded the 2014–15 season, the skies looked blue and bright for Nigel Pearson, regaled as our messiah in glorious May.

You might have thought those skies set fair for him, that years of grace for him did lie in wait. How foolish you'd have been if thought you that. How soon the broody, portentous clouds re-formed.

Now, Nige is not an easy man to love, to those who know him only from afar. Close-up, he's a diamond geezer — couldn't wish for a nicer guy — but few other than his boys get close.

Intemperate when irked he often is, while irked he all too easily seems to be. You recall that February day as relegation loomed, when he placed his mitts around a Palace player's throat? Other eruptions from him there came besides, as happens when the pressure sorely mounts. Let this alone give flavour of his wrath.

After that 1–3 loss to Chelsea's champions elect — the lone defeat in nine post-burial games (just sayin') — off he went on one in conclave with press hacks. It's there on YouTube if you have time to spare. If not, swift told, he had a fearful rant, fixing a scribe with blazing eye, humiliating the wretch before his peers, taunting him for 'ostrich' with head in sand.

Such forthright tongue ill served him with the board, with whom relations had quite awhile been strained. If Nige was already on borrowed time, the fatal loan was truly pound of flesh, for 'twas supplied by his own flesh and blood — 'twas James his son who unwitting wielded the axe.

Yet, hard as 'tis to raise a boy child to manhood, managing a football club is harder.

For to be head coach is to be king, and yet not king. You rule the dressing room, aye, yet another, higher tyrant commands you. Even as the Kings of England once, before bawdy Henry VIII broke the chains, did shiver in the shadow of the Pope.

For 'tis chairman of the club who stands supreme, whose thumb doth rise and fall to seal your fate. And Vichai Srivaddhanaprabha's did for Pearson's doom descend, after the ill-fated club tour to his homeland in the east.

We will linger not upon this tale, for an acrid taste it leaves upon the tongue. 'Tis written in the *Mirror* and the *Sun* (though not the stars, for stellar it was not), so waits online for those who would know more.

One night in June in Vichai's Thai hotel (also King Power by name, and in Bangkok), Pearson's son and others did themselves debase. A trinity of hookers in their teens were ushered to chamber of the bed there to disrobe, then sinuously they did dance for lascivious eyes, and engage in sexing sport betwixt themselves, while James and his two friends did leering watch.

'Twould alone have been enough to cause a stink, for encaptur'd all this was on camera phone. Yet compounded was their sin by manyfold, for they did verbally abuse those dancing girls, with words about the slanting of their eyes, as Edinburgh's Duke did speak in China once, though without the Duke's

21

misplaced attempt at wit.

For Vichai and Aiyawatt Srivaddhanaprabha, not merely chairman's son but his vice chair too, such vice could not imaginably be borne. For they those recent years had worked to increase the traffic of vacationers to their native land, and so the local purse enrich with 'goodwill tours', though no prey did this goodwill hunting run to ground.

'Twas on the 17th day of June that Srivaddhanaprabha patience did expire, and the boy Pearson and the other pair — players at the club, like James, till then — were from Leicester City's books expunged.

How often in myth and history do we find a son raining grief upon his father's name? With the crapulous word-whore Shakespeare 'twas quite a theme, and also with Dr Freud who looked at minds, though mothers and sons seemed more to Sigmund's taste, like Oedipus who Laius at crossroads slew, and in ignorance gave his mum Jocasta a seeing-to.

My own father in truth I barely knew, for he died when I was eight. Probably as well. I'm not saying I'd have done him, as tiny Caligula dispatched noble Germanicus to the underworld. But to be fair — or put another way, in all fairness — you can't rule it out.

And what of Edward, eighth of his name to sit upon England's throne, Nazi manqué, traitor king, who broke George V's heart by frolicking with Maryland's strumpet of whom 'twas said she learned such nether-region tricks in those same bawdy houses of Orient whence our Thai dancing girls did come?

And did you ever see *Thor*, a favourite movie of mine I must confess (loved that flying hammer! Could've done with that at Bosworth), wherein the thunder god did Odin sore distress by warring with the Frost Giants in defiance of the Asgardian sovereign's will.

Boys shalt be boys, or so we used to say, and thus it was in covert days of yore. But in the age of video-camera phone, which captureth the image as it moves, boys at their grave peril be boys, and oft times at the peril of their dads.

Once James Pearson was from the King Power flung, the writing for his sire was 'pon the wall, though perhaps it had been there already a little while, in pencil scrawled if not by inky quill. For Nigel would not lightly kiss the ring, so thus displeased the owners from Siam, or so at least it feels safe to assume.

While the cliché holds it be the case, that for yes-men the powerful hold contempt, the truth could not be more to the obverse. 'Tis sycophants we rulers value most, and those who dare say nay to us we hate. A little life lesson there for you office folk. Make thy tongues as brown as the pelt of a deer roaming the forest in autumn if thou wouldst get on.

With James's dismissal the final straw did come, and on 30 June a club statement issued forth. I quoth the proclamation here verbatim, a touch précis'd only for concision:

> Regrettably, the club believes that the working relationship between Nigel and the board is no longer viable. It has become clear that fundamental differences in perspective exist between us . . . We trust that the supporters will recognise that the owners have always acted with the best interests of the club at heart and with the long-term future as their greatest priority.

This trust of which they spoke was pure phantasm, the fans recognising no such noble intent. To them, 'twas folly to dispense with he who so lately the bonds of hope from doom had forged, and brought on players — our most beloved Vardy, the subtle Mahrez, brave Morgan at the back, those stout English yeomen Albrighton and Drinkwater, whom I would have had at my side at Tewkesbury, and more; to each and every one we'll shortly come — who would ere long be the darlings of the league.

But hark, who comest now with heart in
* which wrath and rage be aflicker?*
Why, it's our onetime Foxes golden boy,
* the crisp salesman Gary Lineker.*

The mellow Lineker had ne'er been so cross since Graham Taylor took him off in that game when he was but one shy of Bobby Charlton's scoring record of forty-nine England goals. Yet at eventide of 30 June, when Pearson's demise had barely yet sunk in, he did tweet forth like an outraged sparrow — and not once, but in quick succession twice.

Gary Lineker
@GaryLineker
Leicester City have sacked Nigel Pearson! Really?
WTF! Could you kindly reinstate him like the last time you fired him?
7:41 PM — 30 Jun 2015

Gary Lineker
@GaryLineker
Getting LCFC promoted and the great-est escape ever, Pearson is sacked? Are

the folk running football stupid? Yes
8:05 PM — 30 Jun 2015

Stupid is as stupid doth, as Mother Gump observed. Reflecting with the hindsight fools revere, though 'tis to wisdom as iron pyrites is to gold, Lineker looks the stupid one today. Yet I would not affect to have felt other than he that day.

WTF? I too thought to myself. (Even though I do LOL at the recollection now!) Why hast thou dispensed with Nige, and who in devil's name will coach us now?

Now, any managerial hiring is like a box of chocolates. Never do you know what you're gonna get. Unless you hire Steve McClaren. Then you know exactly what you're gonna get. Otherwise 'tis a gamble, even as throwing a die three times upon the ground, and hoping each time to see a six.

Yet for too long in this vexing case, the board knew not who they were gonna get.

The brief hiatus between old and new season is an evil time to be bereft of helmsman. War has its close season too, of course, and its transfer window when generals barter for fresh troops.

E'en thus it was when I led white-ros'd
York,

Fearing defection by soldiers with tongues
  of fork,
Who might switch from white to foul
  Lancastrian red —
As Sol Campbell, traitor, left Spurs for
  Arsenal's bed.

The point, my friends, is this. There are players to be sold, players to be loaned in and out, players to be purchas'd from all corners of the world . . . It's a vital time. You can't afford to be without a boss in the close season. That's mental.

With Pearson gone, the Foxes had no boss, though many names were touted for the berth. Sean Dyche of Burnley contended early doors, as did David Moyes who to balmy Sociedad had repaired after being impaled by Manchester United sword (mutual consent my Plantagenet arse).

Many wished that Martin O'Neill, a Foxes manager before, like Pearson be given a second crack. Sam Allardyce was also in the lists, howe'er he be too portly for the joust. So too was Harry Redknapp, from whose eyes shines gospel truth. Yet he had departed QPR but a few months before, citing arthritic soreness in his knee as cause of that, and not the Superhoops' most grievous form, which saw them finish in last place, the twentieth spot not long before earmarked for us. And though Honest Hal did disavow that lame excuse, and claimed that others advanced it unbeknownst to him, even as Shakespeare bestowed false cripplehood on me, the damage to his chances was surely done.

More besides were rumoured for the job, such as Neil Lennon with hair the fading red of flame, and cherubic Eddie Howe who at plucky Bournemouth prospers yet. But whosoe'er was touted was flouted by the board, until Foxes fans muttered in despair, 'Lord have mercy, not Sven-Göran Eriksson again.'

And when at last the choice of boss was made, and the new gaffer was in midst July revealed, 'twas a name that had been spoken of by none.

So great was the shock, the ague did take hold, and tongues that would speak out in rage were stilled, though 'twould be not long ere power of speech returned, and angry birds such as Lineker to Twitter turned.

And this was the consensus when they did, to paraphrase a little if I might.

Oh Jesus wept, no. Not the fucking Tinkerman.

3

. . . LONG LIVE THE KING!

*When raised up to the throne by head of
  steam,*
First test for a new king is e'er the same,
*Be he monarch or coach in the beautiful
  game:*
*Stick glue-like to what is? Or change
  regime?*

Such was the quandary for Claudio Ranieri
when he filled the Pearson void. A Roman,
soft-spoken, antidote to poison of Mourinho,
whose raving paranoia did at Chelsea once
replace his gentle tone.

What was he to do, this incoming boss?
Replace incumbent backroom staff with loyal
lieutenants of his own? Clear out existing
players whose obeisance lay in doubt, hiring
mercenaries to his taste from far and wide?
Or shun revolution's lure in stability's name,
and wait a while to see what need be done?

'Tis by and large the neophyte ruler's way
to erase all that before him was, the easier to
stamp his image 'pon blank page. And not

just in football, come to that. In each and every field 'tis much the same.

Now, take the eighthwit George Walker (President) Bush, chief warlord of the States for eight troubled years. When he did from power remove Saddam Hussein, that Mesopotamian tyrant of bushy 'tache, he and those who yanked Dubya's strings this way and that — Cheney, Rumsfeld, other gangsters of that ilk — did act as arrogant men are fain to do.

They cast the Ba'athists from their crucial task managing that wretch'd strife-torn land, and thus pernicious vacuum did create. Nature abhorring such, it soon was filled, with civil war between Sunni and Shia (who did not serenade the other with love, as near namesakes Sonny and Cher did of yore), and also emboldening that harsh neighbour Iran, until turmoil over the whole region ran amok.

Such monstrous seeds were sown by folly of Bush — aye, and of his grinning, pliant bondsman Tony Blair — that we see a hideous harvest ripening still. All for want of retaining a regime, to stabilise the post-invasion scene.

Ranieri was more sagacious, as we'll see, and perchance therein lay seeds of his success. But before we come to that and other things, a word or two about the cruel greetings that his appointment as Leicester City coach drew forth.

Yon Lineker, of whom we spoke above, did once again give vent to carping chirp, on Twitter where angry birds do flock. 'Claudio Ranieri is clearly experienced,' he piously opined, 'but this is an uninspired choice.' Again his grave mistake I can't condemn, or pretend that I thought otherwise on the day, which was to be exact 13 July. For the hiring did seem as ill-omened as men believe the number thirteen doth portend.

No soothsayer alive was so preposterous skill'd to say the sooth that would later be revealed, as the 2015–16 season began to be unveiled.

For who that gazed into their crystal ball, and sighted Leicester proud atop the league, would not have dashed that ball onto stone floor, smashing it to myriad smithereens, chastising it for rascally orb of glass, which bore false witness to make its owner look an arse?

No one saw this coming, is my point. Not Lineker, not Claudio, not I.

Experienc'd he truly was, as Lineker said, though much of that lay in taking second place, and more in taking leave with pay-off cheque. Seven times already had he been discharged, and thrice resigned himself, and never in all those jobs a single title won.

At Chelsea in tranquil time before Mourinho

came, to rain madness and silverware on Stamford Bridge in equal part, Ranieri three and a half years as coach had spent. His last season encapsulates the gist, with Chelsea runner-up in League and also Cup, in both the prize by but a whisker missed.

Hence 'Nearly Man' was one of his nicknames, with 'Tinkerman' the other sobriquet, for his penchant for e'er rotating his squad, and being unable his best eleven to say. Seldom twice on the bounce the same side did he pick, though by and by that habit would he break.

To his Chelsea stint a Croesus brought an end, the oligarch Abramovich by name, a Roman yet no Roman like Ranieri he, but came from the vast wastes of Russia's icy steppe. Great treasure had he found in mysterious way, after into the abyss the Soviets collapsed. He spent a portion of his gold to buy the Blues, and more — much more — to make them glister once again.

And after more than thirty years of being bored into a coma (not me, of course, being dead already; 'tis but a figure of speech) by Chelsea fans yacking on and on about the 1970 FA Cup final — Peter Osgood this, Charlie Cooke that, David Webb's shouldering the fucking winner in the Old Trafford replay against Don Revie's Leeds — the revival came as some relief. Now at last they had some fresh vainglorious drivel to spout.

Yet Claudio, being kind and full of smile, was not Abramovich's type of guy. The Russian hired José Mourinho from Porto in his stead, and soon enough Chelsea champions became. Back then in the year of our lord 2005, who would have believed this reversal a decade hence — which of them would this year get the sack, and which as coaching genius be wide acclaimed?

Yet even as Mourinho his stellar reputation built, winning the Champions League in nations twain, and many league titles and domestic cups besides, Ranieri collected little but the boot.

Which clubs (and country) sacked Ranieri. Aye, and when:
Napoli: 1993
Chelsea: 2004
Valencia: 2005
Juventus: 2009
Inter Milan: 2012
Monaco: 2014
Greece: 2014

That he was lately twice fired within a year tended ill for Leicester City, or so we thought. Especially when he ended his stay in

Greece by putting the hell (and what hell!) into Hellenic.

To lose one Euro 2016 qualifier to the Faroes may as misfortune be regarded, though an unconscionable misfortune at that. These are not the Pharaohs, mind, to spell it out for the word blind, or 'dyslexics' as I think they're known today. No disgrace in losing to the descendants of Cleopatra who with Marc Antony lay — and who, according to one buffoonish bard, an asp to her alabaster bosom took. To such Pharaohs you could lose with pride intact.

I speak instead of an archipelago of sparse-peopled rocks, marooned alone in the North Atlantic ocean, under dominion of Denmark whence our beloved Kasper Schmeichel came.

To lose once to such Faroes is woe indeed, but may be written off as one of them things.

To lose twice, and not over years but in a trice — 'tis truly Greek to me, how such a thing could be. Under Ranieri in but months it came to pass, both home and away, and ousted from his Grecian throne he was, as King Constantine was removed by the Colonels some decades before.

Who then could have foreseen that this, his lowest point, would be the launchpad for vertiginous ascent? But perhaps 'tis smaller surprise than it may seem.

For when what seems worst misfortune
   rears its head,
Oft times 'tis naught but blessing in
   disguise.
And those who can discern with piercing
   eyes
See not past calamity, but undream'd
   future glory in its stead.

A word of credit belongs to chairman and his
son, Vichai and Aiyawatt Srivaddhanaprabha,
who land on King Power turf in whirly metal-
lic bird, the helicopter da Vinci once foresaw,
and when the game is done leave the same way.
A bit flash, to be sure, but none the worse for
that, so long as they can spare the cash.

These Thailanders might well have been
offput by the double disaster at Faroe Islands'
hands. Yet they were impress'd by interviews
in which the Roman advanced his claim, and
spoke of what as Leicester coach he'd do.
And in better English than in his Chelsea
days, when interpreters to the training ground
did throng, to translate what he had to tell his
lads.

And what Claudio told the Siamese he'd
do, was next to nothing in the short term. For
here we see the brilliance of the man, that
when he might have changed the old regime,
he stuck like glue to pre-existing team.

The backroom staff stayed on to smooth his path, including Nigel Pearson's number two, Craig Shakespeare, whose name speaks naught but dread to me, as to anyone likewise sore besmirch'd by odious and malevolent verse that libels us as murderers and rogues.

Then again, if all were judged by predecessor's name, they'd call me Lion Heart like Richard I, not cowardly, scheming, crookback snake.

This present Shakespeare had been with the Foxes seven years, joining as Nigel Pearson's assistant in 2008, and was integral to the running of the team, as Ranieri appeared to appreciate. Also retained was our leading scout Steve Walsh, whose part in this tale cannot be overlooked, for he, far-sighted goose, laid golden eggs by finding Jamie Vardy at Fleetwood, scenting greatness in him low in non-league though he was, as a pig sniffs priceless truffle in midst of mud and earth.

And not Vardy alone. He also found Riyad Mahrez, did Stevey Walsh, wasted in the French division two, and purchased him for trifling amount from Le Havre on Normandy coast. And the Austrian left back Christian Fuchs, another in our firmament of stars, anonymous in Bundesliga then, at Schalke, where Walshy saw something to intrigue, and on a free transfer did snaffle him forthwith.

Ere Ranieri's appointment was confirmed, more jigsaw pieces were already put in place. From Japan, land of the rising sun, came Shinji Okazaki, a striker and an acrobat as well, as he did later prove with overhead kick, who also came from a club in Germany, the homeland of our granite Robert Huth. Huth himself had come in February from Stoke, on loan until the season's startling end. But in early July, before Ranieri came, he signed for good for some three million quid.

What Ranieri did by way of trade, in two short weeks before the new season commenced, was sign N'Golo Kanté from Caen — a precious midfield gem, whether driving forward to help the lads up front, or racing back to rescue his defence.

And there, bar one or two trivial dealings, Ranieri was content to cease from trade, and leave the transfer window to slide shut, until January's reopening at least.

So to his first meeting with his chaps, for here it may be said the Rubicon was crossed, and the future embark'd upon if not yet set in stone. Or as that dunce Shakespeare hath me say, in that scandalous pile of pus that bears my name:

I have set my life upon a cast,
And I will stand the hazard of the die.

37

The lads were not entire enamour'd, at first, of the plans the Roman posited for them. He wished to alter how they trained, and what they ate, and the tactics which they used on field of play.

One senior man whose name we do not know — a spokesman for his fellows, not just himself — set out at once to set the gaffer straight. He explained that the recent melodramatic escape (seven games won of nine when all looked lost — and as I may also have pointed out once or twice before, following my reinterment beneath cathedral floor) came after Pearson chose to relax his yoke, and free them that they might express themselves.

Respectfully the request was issued forth, that Ranieri follow his predecessor's path, and not plot out their every waking move, as Italian coaches — neurotic micromanagers! — are far too wont to do.

Now, thinking back to my time at the helm as head coach of England FC, if you will, I don't think I'd have taken such a petition with grace. 'Tis not a subject's business, after all, to tell a king how he should make plans.

If a counsellor had come to me within days of my coronation saying, 'Gaffer' ('twas not a form of address in currency then, yet I like its earthy, uncouth ring) — if he'd looked me in the eye and said, 'Gaffer, don't take offence or nuffink, or not, but we liked it better before under your noble brother, Edward IV. We beg you, sire, to reconsider, and leave all as it was . . . ' Look, I'm not saying I'd have had the insolent cur carted off to the Tower and disappeared, because that was ne'er my mode of business, as you know. But nor do I say that I would such a courtier's life insurer be, nor yet place a deposit in silver coin to secure the banqueting chamber for his retirement party years hence.

Yet Ranieri took the intervention in good heart, and more than that did listen to these words, and acceded in whole to that request, to leave things as they were before he came.

Who can say what rival fate lay in store, if he had imposed his will upon the squad, and abandoned the *modus operandi* with which Pearson launched ascent from table's foot, thus setting them on the road they latterly took, which none can scarce believe unto this day?

As it goes, I'm no fan of counterfactual history. All that speculating about what if . . .

What if Catherine of Aragon had borne Henry VIII a son, and England had remained under Vatican yoke? What if the yellow taxi cab which knocked down Winston Churchill in New York, years before the Second World War began, had killed him, rather than merely busting up a leg? In that event, would more Foxes than Huth and Fuchs speak German fluently?

Who gives one, hmm? Kings perforce must deal with what is, not waste time on what might have been but wasn't. It's a bit fey, the alternative timeline stuff. A shade too *Sliding Doors* for me.

Yet however loath to dwell on times that never were, I cannot help but ponder what might have been, had Ranieri been tyrannical of heart, and tied in chains those who would be free.

Another relegation scrap? Mid-table respectability? Whatever befell us then, it could not have been what is. So give thanks for a man who knows what ears are for, and also that he knows not all himself.

Our Claudio makes as unlikely a Roman god as Claudius, the emperor mentioned above who at birth seemed as ill-formed to rule as me, yet overcame his lameness in the end, and when he died a deity was declared.

When finally he departs this mortal coil, many years from now, as all men must, Ranieri too shall be deified as is his right.

To Greece he shall return, to sit with
    Jove and Juno,
Making sport 'mongst gods as once he
    did on earth.
And if Olympians FC need a coach, he'll
    fill that berth.
(Ne'er saw that coming when interr'd
    'neath Y-reg Fiat Uno.)

4

SO IT BEGINS

As a poet — not that one — once wisely
*   spake*
('Tis wrongly sourc'd to that pustulous
*   Stratford bane,*
As others' wit is oft times misattributed
*   to Twain):*
'Expectation is the root of all heartache.'

We can all appreciate the truth of that, but especially the followers of Chelsea FC (hahaha-haha). For as the summer fruits ripened upon the trees, they had great expectation of retaining their title — and nothing but heartache lay in store for them.

And what of we who with the Foxes walk each step ('Everywhere we go/We make the gang go/Leicester! Leicester!!')? Despite the dramatic change in fortunes at previous season's end, our expectations for the next were exceeding low.

Two days afore the fresh campaign began, the gaffer issued a warning to us fans, although we, arch realists, needed none.

'Claudio Ranieri has warned Leicester they face an even bigger fight to survive this season,' the Sky Sports online site related. 'The Foxes pulled off a great escape last season, winning seven of their final nine games to stay up under Nigel Pearson . . . Ahead of the season opener, the Italian said his side must be prepared for another scrap. 'The Premier League is very hard, we are a little team . . . In my career I've seen it is more difficult in the Premier League in the second year than the first year.''

And with glum Claudio the bookmakers did concur, as a glance at the odds against us going down, and also at those for winning the Premier League, will instantly confirm. In fact you will see that the drop was regarded as a likelier prospect than taking the title by a thousandfold and more.

Pre-season odds on Premier League relegation, 2015–16
Watford 4–6
Norwich 1–1
Bournemouth 11–8
Sunderland 15–8
Aston Villa 5–2
Leicester 3–1
West Brom 9–2
Newcastle 5–1

West Ham 7–1
Crystal Palace 8–1
Swansea 11–1
Stoke 16–1

Pre-season odds on Premier League champions, 2015–16
Chelsea 13–8
Manchester City 5–2
Arsenal 4–1
Manchester Utd 5–1
Liverpool 28–1
Tottenham 100–1
Southampton 200–1
Everton 250–1
Stoke 1,500–1
Swansea 1,500–1
Crystal Palace 2,000–1
West Ham 2,500–1
Aston Villa 5,000–1
Bournemouth 5,000–1
Leicester 5,000–1
Newcastle 5,000–1
Norwich 5,000–1
Sunderland 5,000–1
Watford 5,000–1
West Brom 5,000–1

Even this gives but the wispiest flavour of the size of the miracle we will forever savour. It just happens to be that 5,000–1 is the longest price any rapscallion bookie will e'er quote.

Pop into Wllm Hill and request the odds about anything — Donald J. Trump being appointed Andrea Dworkin Professor of Neo-Feminist Studies at Yale; Eric Pickles being cast as the new James Bond; or Madonna, bless her, being crowned Celebrity Mum of the Year. Me, come to that, becoming posthumous Celebrity Uncle of the Year (but on those unexplain'd vanishings let us not dwell) — and 5,000–1 is the most you will e'er be offered.

Katie Price having a maidenhead regraft to seize the mantle of the virginal Mother Teresa, and taking the 2020 Nobel Peace Prize (never underestimate the Pricey, mayhap, but even so . . .)? 5,000–1!

Stevie Wonder winning the Malaysian Grand Prix at the wheel of Margaret Beckett's caravan? 5,000–1!

Victoria Beckham emerging from a display of comely original fashions on David's arm, grinning for the cameras like Wet Wet Wet rictus sufferer Marti Pellow (he who feeleth it in his fingers; aye, and in his toes) on triple rations of nitrous oxide? 5,000–1!

The true odds of becoming champions, I estimate, were closer to 1,000,000–1, and closest of all to infinity–1. Winning the league was an event that could not be; a cast-iron impossibility.

But enough of the prologue, ladies and gents, and transgenders too, for 'tis time to raise the curtain upon our mystery play.

★ ★ ★

'Twas upon 8 August, the eighth of the eighth for those who care about such things, whether believing the number lucky like the Chinese, or dreading its approach like myself, a fretful octophobe, that the new season kicked off with Sunderland welcomed to the King Power.

Now sportingfolk are superstitious types, with a myriad of rituals to perform (think of Rafa Nadal tugging his knickers from his crack afore and after each and every point).

So too were we medieval kings, who did on battle's eve the auspices inspect, searching them for signs of good and bad. The black cat was a hateful portent in my time, a dreaded witchy creature tending ill, and so to this day it doth remain. Yet for us on the eighth of the eighth, the Black Cats proved the luckiest of charms.

The game embarked at three that afternoon, and before the clock chimed the half hour, by three were we ahead. It fell to Jamie

Vardy, lean and lion-hearted, to get this party started, heading home a Marc Albrighton free kick with eleven minutes gone. Only seven more had passed when Riyad Mahrez, also with his head, a second scored. After seven more went by, the same man secured a third from penalty spot.

They pulled one back in the second half afore Albrighton scored our fourth, and eventually a 4–2 victory was secured. By dint of more goals scored, we led the league that night. And though that table looked a mirage to us then, 'twould prove a verdant oasis glimmering from afar.

And what of Chelsea, those cockily expectant Blues? Strife and mayhem at Stamford Bridge them befell, for they had a man sent off vs Swansea in a flukey 2–2 draw. Think not that I smile as I compose these words, for 'tis not a prince's style with *Schadenfreude* to gloat, even about a raving Portugueser madman who had replaced Ranieri some ten full years before. But for José Mourinho, as for King Belshazzar in the scriptural tale, the writing was on the wall.

A week went by and to east London we processed, to play West Ham at their now abandoned Upton Park, or Boleyn Ground as it was formerly known, after that 'goggle-eyed whore' Anne, queen to Henry VIII until she lost her head, though it took scant effort to lop it away, for as she told her French axeman, 'I have only a little neck.' Yes, yes, I've read Hilary Mantel too.

To West Ham, as to us, the summer had a new king brought, in the lean Croatian form of Slaven Bilić, vulpine of feature yet no Fox he, a villainous footballer of yore, who by clutching his face for no apparent cause did frame poor Laurent Blanc for assault in the World Cup semi of 1998, and by thus enticing red card from the ref, had the Frenchman banned from the final match. Not that it did much the French to vex. Blancless, they crushed Brazil by a scoreline of 3–0.

Yet I digress.

'Twas brass-necked Bilić who this day lost his head, while Shinji Okazaki used his to good effect, heading home our first goal afore too long, his first for us since signing in July. This Japanese pleased his strike partner more than some. For in the days before the game, Jamie Vardy had been fined and censured after a tabloid reported a casino mishap, whereby he crossly addressed a gambler from Nippon by the rude and charmless diminutive of 'Jap'.

'Twas not the first time Vardy gave offence, as we'll see in a chapter dedicated to him hence. But while this confers on them no defence, young men are oft short on common sense. Okazaki was quick to say that he, as a Japanese, took no offence. From their embrace after he scored the first against West Ham, that seemed the truth and no mere mannerly pretence.

Before half time our slender lead was doubled, when Okazaki released Albrighton down the left, and Mahrez swept his pinpoint cross into the net. West Ham halved their deficit in the second period of play, with a goal nimbly taken by Dimitri Payet, who is to the Hammers' midfield what Mahrez is to ours (a godly genius). But stoutly we clung on for a 2–1 win, and thus did remain atop the league, if only until the Sabbath came next day, when by Liverpool, Crystal Palace and Man City we were leapfrogged.

When the following game, our third, was played at home, the omens for me were melancholy and obscene. For Spurs came to play on 22 August, by far the most pernicious date of all. That was the day in 1485 on which I was scythed down at Bosworth Field, and duly died.

I hope you've come to know me well enough, in the course of these splendid pages I have writ, to feel a pang of pity that I did snuff, so young and in excruciating pain. Then again, or so we may suppose, had I survived and won that War of Rose, and remained upon my throne awhile yet, I would in full time have died elsewhere, and never beneath a Leicester council car park been left, nor ever dug up and in a cathedral relaid to rest, less than a mile from King Power where we play. And who in that event could say that Leicester City would have been so blest? Just asking.

Fitting enough in this miasma of doubt, over whether my death day was a portent good or ill, the match with Spurs (which prefaced long combat to come) ended without a win for either side. Two goals and only two were scored, both late and in a madcap, headlong rush. The first from Dele Alli, precocious lad, with ten minutes left; the equaliser, within a minute and half, by a Mahrez left-foot shot.

The following Saturday took us to Hampshire coast, to newly risen Bournemouth's Dean Court home, where the scoreline was as it was 'gainst the Spurs — another 1–1 draw, in other words, and again by skin of teeth. The Cherries led from midway through first half, and cleaved to their advantage near the end. With bare four minutes of normal time to play, plus whatever the officials would see fit to append, Vardy charged into the Bournemouth box, where he induced a tackle mistim'd and rash. The ref, God spare him, pointed to the spot, and Jamie himself stepped up to make net bulge.

Now why, you ask, did Vardy take that pen, and not Mahrez who scored that earlier spot kick? It happened that our well-loved Moor had not excelled that day, and was removed as early as half time, which did much credit to the boss, who felt that if a change was to be made, 'twere best done quick, so sent on Okazaki in Mahrez's stead for entire second half.

Yet if this altering the structure of his team suggests to you the Tinkerman of old, nothing could be further from the truth. For as the season did unravel, Ranieri along the tinker's path refused to travel, using fewer players in fact than any other coach.

When Man City won their fourth game on the trot, while we had two wins and two draws, we trailed them by a full quartet of points, though 'twas of course the earliest of doors.

How we won when next we played at home is an enigma to this day, for Aston Villa led us 2–0 late on, and appeared guaranteed to pocket all three points. Yet perchance the knack of cheating death, as acquired from our great escape the previous spring, had seeped into Leicester City's DNA. Now, when defeat appeared our certain fate, it fell to Mahrez to turn things on their head. It seemed his early bath the previous week had restored him to his most majestic best, as he conducted the tempo of our play like the lustrous Moorish maestro that he is.

First, up from the back for a Leicester corner kick, and with about eighteen minutes remaining in the game, our Belgian defender Ritchie De Laet scrambled home, though the ball barely crossed the Bournemouth line at all, requiring goal-line video technology to make the goodly call.

Ten minutes later the equaliser came, when Vardy slammed home a Danny Drinkwater cross. On and on we surged in a feverish foaming tide, which at the death could no longer be repelled. In the final seconds before closing whistle blew, delirium shook the King Power from root to branch, when tiny Nathan Dyer found some way to loop a gorgeous Mahrez pass into the net.

Dyer stands at only five feet five, which was no great height even in my time, when nutrition frankly wasn't up to much. He signed in August, just moments before the transfer window closed, on loan from Swansea until season's end, being another apparent misfit in our squad, like Albrighton whom Aston Villa had neglected on the bench, and Vardy who at Fleetwood had languished so long, and others beside to whom we'll come anon — disregarded as irrelevant pygmies by their clubs, and given away or sold for a penny piece to Leicester, where into titans they metamorphosed.

'Tis a lesson worth the learning, is it not, that in football as in a children's fairy tale, an ugly duckling may grow into a swan; and that coin alone cannot glory secure, there being so much more to life than treasure's lure.

But I get ahead of myself. For the moment be it sufficient to behold the early autumnal table, truncated a jot, showing Leicester loftily placed, and Chelsea most hilariously adrift.

Premier League table on 14 September 2015

Pos	Team	P	GD	Pts
1	Man City	5	11	15
2	Leicester City (!)	5	4	11
3	Man United	5	3	10
4	Arsenal	5	2	10
5	West Ham	5	5	9
6	Crystal Palace	5	2	9
17	Chelsea (!!!)	5	-5	4
18	Stoke City	5	-4	2
19	Sunderland	5	-5	2
20	Newcastle	5	-5	2

It maketh pretty reading, doth it not, though it remained too soon to succumb to expectation, with consequent risk of grievous heartache ahead.

> So far, so good — yet still, who thought
>   we'd win it?
> And who that did, to such hubris confess'd,
> Adapting Miranda's line in The Tempest:
> 'O brave new world, that has such champ-
>   ions in it'?

5

AND WHAT A PARTY!

*Whippet-lean, in no wise a bucket of
lard, he*
*From non-league came, a gift from
football's gods.*
*Pre-eminent among our odds, and aye,
our sods,*
*I speak, as you'll have guessed, of Jamie
Vardy.*

I, Richard Plantagenet, Duke of Gloucester, Lord Protector, King, third and last of my name to sit upon the throne . . . I, Richard of England, am no more given to fanciful literary chit-chat than to listing my titles in braggardly array. It's just not who I am. *Capisce?*

Yet when I think of this book — of what has been assigned to pages past, and what shall be on pages yet to come — I detect the stirrings of a 'theme'; a morality play, if you will, within which may be found lessons about the meandering, unchartable river that is human fate.

For the tale I tell is not simply one of events so far beyond prognosticating that none — not Cassandra of Troy, not Tiresias of Thebes, not Nostradamus of Provence, not Mystic Meg of the *Sun* — could have scented their approach upon the wind.

It is also the story of how those written off as failures can — if the dice fall well, and if they have the gumption to ride their luck — storm into the vanguard.

'Twas my own story long ago. Whelped a sickly babe, reared a wan and feeble boy condemn'd to skulk in shadows while my brothers basked in sunlight, I by courage and native wit did cheat suppos'd destiny, and seize the crown.

So who shall condemn me if I wax lachrymose with pride as I consider how my boys made what is known to Simon Cowell, high-trousered *meister* of the tone-deaf, liege lord of the Maria Carey wannabe, as 'an amazing, amazing journey'? How they came to live perchance the dream?

Marc Albrighton, that stallion who doth charge without fear, was mistook by Aston Villa — fools, fools, who gave him away one season, and would the next have given the very earth to have him back — for a mule.

Behold, beside Albrighton in midfield, Danny Drinkwater, who pulls the strings, a marvellous puppeteer; yet whom Man Utd never once for first team picked, selling him to us for an undisclosed fee, believed to be half a groat, or in the vicinity.

And what of Kasper Schmeichel, whom Man City passed to lowly Leeds — Schmeichel, son of Schmeichel, with a shining future in his past before he to Leicester came, and was reborn a blond Norse god between the sticks?

More renaissances than these have we seen, yet none echoes so sweetly as the resurrection song of Jamie Vardy, who was buried in a catacomb of irrelevance — as was I myself in that fucking council car park.

Now some, gazing at Jamie's visage, do note a striking resemblance to my own. And in sooth there is about that hard and whippety face a hint of the angular, merciless Plantagenet boat race. 'Tis not a fizzog 'pon which thou wouldst chance, after spilling a pint of Stella upon his crotch at a lairy Leicester disco dance. Or indeed, as we will learn anon, outside a boozer when a skinful hath by all been taken.

Yond Vardy, like Cassius in the Avon ponce's play, hath a lean and hungry look. Such men are dangerous. I know it well, for I was such a man, and dangerous was I to they who blocked my path, as Vardy is to those who would block his route to goal.

Percipient reader, you will detect that in this boy a shadow of myself I discern, wondering whether in him there be a bit of me. And I am not talking metaphorically.

Only one armed with a DNA testing kit, taking a hair from Vardy's head and a scraping of my bone, could say for certain whether portion of my genes was passed along in love's juddering embrace — and on again, and on and on as centuries elapsed, and all the way to him.

This much I know. Vardy is a son of Yorkshire, like me, and slid into this world in Sheffield, on 11 January 1987. 'Twas no fine time to be born, for the forging of steel was dying at the hand of Thatcher, the latterday Boadicea who manufacturing industry crushed beneath the patent-leather piledriver that was her handbag.

Thou must have seen the entertainment *The Full Monty*, set at exactly the time of Vardy's birth, wherein unfortunate men laid off from defunct steelworks did seek to supplement their paltry dole, their vestments saucily discarding to flaunt their dangling privy parts at women cheering in ribald disbelief to the sound of a Hot Chocolate number one.

Now come on, everybody, sing along with Little Richard (III):

I believe in miracles,
Since you came along.
Jamie Vardy,
You sexy thing!
You sexy thang!

For is it not indeed miraculous that Vardy, unesteemed as he was, did soar to greatness at an age when men are more usually rooted to the spot?

Ian Wright was likewise one among so few, being well into his twenties when he broke through from non-league obscurity — and then only after a brief brush with the law, Wrighty doing a fortnight's bird for driving uninsured, weeping in his cell and promising the Lord that on release he would do all he might, his potential to fulfil.

And fulfil it Wrighty did, the lovable schlub, first as fearsome striker for club and country, thence as adorable pundit on radio and TV, alongside our own Foxes legend Gary Lineker, the pair together marvelling at Leicester's rise upon *Match of the Day.*

Now, Vardy as a youth was errant too, and at nineteen was up before the beak for an incident in drink outside an inn. The justices did convict him of assault, and though a spell in jug they spared the lad, they obliged him to wear an electronic tag which clung fast to his ankle for six months. For that half year he was under strict curfew, and must be home before evening clock struck six. So when he played for Stocksbridge Park Steels, of Barnsley not far from Sheffield in South Yorks, and a match took place at a distance from his home, he needs must depart the pitch ere full time in order to ensure he made it back afore the tag would beep to alert his local nick.

Looking back three years afore then, at sixteen he was heartrendingly let go by Sheffield Wednesday, his local team, who judged him too small to succeed, and from their academy him callously released.

'Twas like unto a blade in the heart of one so young, and for a time he would not play the game in any form. Not once in eight months did he lace a boot, until the sportive lure proved too strong to resist, and he turned out in the sort of Sunday league wherein men each Sabbath their hangovers ignore.

Soon enough by Stocksbridge he was signed, and so began to play in Northern Premier League, though he also had a day job to discharge, for a non-league player receives but a mean stipend, which he must augment with less appealing work. He put in long, fatiguing shifts lugging heavy boxes in a plant where artificial limbs were from carbon fibre wrought.

Excepting the prosthetics he did help to create, there was nothing false about the combative young cub, for he ran his heart out for his non-league team, e'en as he doth for us today. Yet his advancement was devilish slow to come.

In the summer of 2010 he moved, though remaining still within the Northern Premier League, to Halifax Town, and for a paltry fifteen grand — a fraction of what he now takes home each week. A year on, and to the Conference he rose, the fifth highest of all the English leagues, spending a two-year spell with Fleetwood Town, not many miles from Blackpool's fleshpots. Finally his talent caught the eye of Steve Walsh, our far-sighted head scout, who saw something that tempted him to flout the previous transfer record for non-league, and pay a million quid to snap him up.

Thus in the summer of 2012 Vardy became a Leicester man, and finally it began.

Slowly it began, if truth be told, for his scoring form at first was hardly hot, nor even lukewarm, but freezing cold. Some fans — not I! not I! — had a right old go at him on social media sites wherein the embittered and demented unleash their private rages.

More sensitive than he may perhaps appear, Vardy took such abuse sorely to heart, and after his first season had elapsed, in deep despair he thought to leave the club. Yet Nigel Pearson talked him out of that, with help from his assistant Craig Shakespeare, who performs the same role for Ranieri still. Craig's surname strikes my ears as most unseemly, for it implants the notion that he hath a bard for antecedent (even as Vardy may have a measure of me in his blood) — a pigeon-liver'd poet, carping and shrill, who with venomous quill made wicked a goodly English king.

But enough — more than enough — of repugnant Will, and back to our number nine, whom Pearson and S*********e coaxed with soothing refrain, and persuaded to remain. And thank heaven that they did, for the next season was a triumph for the kid, who scored sixteen times as we eased to promotion, and was anointed our Players' Player of the Season.

The season following, back in Premier League, was troublesome in sooth, as you all know, with Leicester apparently doomed to plunge below — bottom at Yuletide, bottom still in March, when a bag of crooked bones was reinterr'd a mile from the ground. At which point all began to turn around.

Yet even in those dismal months of gloom

Vardy had moments of bliss, such as in September 2014 when he scored one and made all other four, as we stunned Man Utd 5–3 at the Power. And in April 2015, when the escape was well begun, he scored late winners vs Burnley and then West Brom. But although he ended the season in sizzling form, no hint was there of what was soon to come.

Nor was there a sign on the seventh day of June, when he debuted for England against Ireland, replacing Wayne Rooney in a tedious scoreless draw.

Nor could a glimpse of the bejewelled future be seen on 29 August 2015, when his equaliser at Bournemouth launched what was to be a record-setting run. Nor yet when in our next game, that absolute thriller, he scored the second as we came from 2–0 down to beat the Villa.

His third scoring game in succession came in another dogged refusal to surrender, this time to Mark Hughes' doughty Stoke City, whom we trailed by two when half-time whistle blew, before a Mahrez penalty cut the arrears in twain, and Vardy equalised with twenty minutes to go.

Seven days later our first defeat of the season — delayed until late September, hard as that is to believe — was dealt by Arsène

Wenger's Arsenal, who oft times flatter to deceive, looking every inch the champs till pressure mounts, whereupon they find some novel way to fall apart. That day they took us to the cleaners, Vardy scoring a brace either side of their five, as we were dismantled by five to two.

We would not be vanquished again in Premier League until Boxing Day, aka the Feast of Stephen. From now until then, 'twas solely the Feast of Jamie.

After the Gunners reverse we went to Norwich, and sent those canaries down a deep and doomsome pit, besting them by two goals to their one. Vardy fired the first from penalty spot (regular taker Riyad Mahrez being unpicked, the Moor's form then not being so hot), after himself being rudely upended within the box.

At Southampton, comeback kings exactly as at Stoke were we, once again trailing 2–0 when half-time whistle blew, and once again concluding the match tied at 2–2, with Vardy bagging another pair. 'Twas now six games in a row that he had scored, as only three Premier League players this century had done before. He was also now top scorer in the division.

Had you predicted that three years afore, in Fleetwood times, imagine the derision. I'd have had you locked up in the Tower (just my jest; I'd merely have sent you to Bedlam), and thrown away the key!

Next to King Power, as lambs unto the slaughter, came Crystal Palace, whom we felt we surely must beat, if the league table be any kind of guide — though not by much, since only a single point and a single place split the sides. Jamie put away the solitary goal upon the hour, to decide a game that tended to the dour.

There was nothing soporific 'bout what followed next, when westerly to The Hawthorns we progressed. West Brom went ahead on the half hour, but Mahrez struck twice and Vardy added another, this 3–2 victory raising us to third in all the league.

Our opponents next were the hornets of Watford FC, who were conquered at the Power by the odd goal in three, the winner coming from another Vardy penalty.

In nine consecutive games now had Jamie scored, and thus he was but one short of the all-time record as it then did stand — ten successive matches, set in 2003 by Ruud van Nistelrooy, that horse-faced son of Netherland.

Off we went to St James' Park, home of Newcastle United, where to the misery of many a proud Geordie the first of an unanswered trio was scored by Vardy, which saw him equal the record of he who by his visage palpably belonged (no offence) in a stable. Apart from that, by way of afterthought, the win put us on top of the table.

I can see the goal in mind's eye as I write, Jamie picking up a pass from Leonardo Ulloa, a surname I'm told is pronounced as 'Oo-Joe-ah'. You'd have thought we had enough double L nonsense from the good folk of Wales, whence our hated Tudor foes as marauding savages came, though I suppose a J sounds less barbarous than 'ccchhhhhhcccchhhhhllllll', as in Llewellyn or Llandudno, or whate'er.

The said Ulloa hails from a silver-laden southern land, undiscover'd when I was alive, known within football for a satanic 'Hand of God'.

'Twas with a godly foot at St James' Park that Vardy took Ulloa's pass, and twisting this way and that within the Magpies' box, a little space he thieved as magpies will, and fired low inside the near post.

'It is fantastic,' Ranieri told gathered reporters, referring to another Argentine in support of his striker's hope to emulate a great. 'I had Gabriel Batistuta at Fiorentina score in eleven consecutive matches, and I hope Jamie can achieve this.' Didn't we all, mate?

Aye, and more than hoped. For we did pray

that Vardy's run would endure, on 28 November when van Nistelrooy's erstwhile team visited the King Power for a lunchtime game screened live upon BT.

The boots Vardy wore that day against Man U were gold, and so they bleeding well ought to have been.

Some twenty-three minutes had scorelessly elapsed, when Man Utd took a corner on their right. Schmeichel, our keeper, caught the ball with ease, and speedily rolled it out, as oft he does, to cherished full back Christian Fuchs. He unchallenged ran for some twenty-five yards, before threading a perfectly weighted ball — a 'slide-rule pass', in venerable cliché of the game — to Vardy in space on the right side of their box, whence he languidly slotted home, and wheeled away to caper before our delirious fans ere by his fellows he was mobbed as he deserved.

Well, would you credit it? I scarce did, and scarce do now, for as the rhyme below wisely implies, this change in fortune — like so many aspects of the tale told herein — doth bankrupt all belief.

To think that he who eighteen months
* afore near flounced*
Away from Leicester, umbraged at social
* media*

(Doubt that? Then check thy Wikipedia) —
That he now scored in eleven on the bounce!

6

AS ONE DOTH RISE,
SO DOTH ANOTHER FALL

*Delicious tidings of a Ranieri enemy of
   old,*
*Who fell after the two at King Power
   jousted,*
*Long years since from Chelsea he Claudio
   ousted.*
*Doth not revenge taste best when 'tis served
   cold?*

The enemy of whom I speak, as if you
required telling, is that insolent Iberian, that
loud-mouthed Lusitanian lunatic, that petu-
lant Portuguese paranoiac who goes by the
name of José Mourinho. (None of your lip
about the vulgarity of alliteration, thanking
you kindly. Check out *Romeo and Juliet*, or
even one of his mimsy sonnets, and you'll see
it's good enough for your blessed bard.)

Than between Ranieri and Mourinho, no
starker contrast in Latin archetypes may
anywhere be found. The one, serene and full
of politesse, sweet of manner, gentle of voice,

twinklesome of eye, a darling among men. The other . . . not so much.

'Tis not a princely proclivity to grin, jackal-like, when an arrow of outrageous misfortune pierces a man's chainmail and deals that man death. You will meet nothing here that may be paraphrased as 'Nurr-nurr-nur-nurr-nurrrrggggghhhhh!'

Yet 'twould be deception to gainsay the frisson of pleasure that seeped through cathedral floor to my tomb when tidings spread abroad that Mourinho had, for a second time, been binned by Roman Abramovich, the Siberian tiger in human guise who Chelsea doth own.

How much satisfaction Ranieri took from his tormentor's fall, if any at all, none knows. When asked, he said none — and Claudio is an honourable man, which I say without the colicky sarcasm employ'd by Marc Antony of Brutus.

Yet who can see so deep and so clear into another's soul that nothing is obscured, when oft times we blind ourselves e'en to what lies hidden in our own? 'Know thyself,' the Delphic Oracle instructed, yet few have it in them to obey. Not all can have the sublime self-awareness of King Richard III, now can they?

Before we consider the exquisite poetic

justice whereby it fell to Claudio to deliver the lethal blow to one who had so often stabbed at him, a reminder of where we stood as the final month of the year 2015 began.

Jamie Vardy having accomplished that glorious feat of scoring in eleven straight games (only one of which, to Royal Arsenal, we lost), the Foxes entered December in second place, and that on goal difference alone.

Premier League table, duly abridged, on 1 December 2015

Pos	Team	P	GD	Pts
1	Man City	14	16	29
2	Leicester City	14	8	29
3	Man Utd	14	10	28
4	Arsenal	14	12	27
5	Tottenham H	14	13	25
6	Liverpool	14	3	23
14	Chelsea (!!!)	14	-6	15

With but six points separating the leading half-dozen, the pinnacle was as crowded as Mount Everest, where phalanxes of tourists now foregather to cheapen the feats of Hillary and Tenzing, ascending to that global zenith as if climbing a staircase, there discarding

71

their crisp packets and Coke cans that their hands might be free to take selfies at the rooftop of the world. How times do change!

And how quickly they had changed for both hero and villain of this chapter. When this season began, the solitary race for which Ranieri was favourite was that to be first to be sacked. (In the event this honour was shared by Dick Advocaat of Sunderland and Liverpool's Brendan Rodgers, both of whom got the boot on 4 October.)

Those same turf accountants made Mourinho warm favourite to retain the Premier League title he had won the year before whilst barely breaking a sweat. And now, four short months after he vaingloriously lifted that trophy, his tenure at Chelsea hung by a gossamer thread.

Before Ranieri deployed his manicure scissors, he took Leicester City to Swansea on 5 December. And there, in the land of the dragon, Vardy breathed goalscoring fire no more. Instead he graciously took a supporting role, leaving it to our wizardly Moor to fill the hole. And plug the scoring gap Riyad Mahrez assuredly did, helping himself to a splendid hat-trick, the first with his head when but five minutes had passed, the next not long after (when, truth to tell, offside he appeared), the third coming midway through the second half. With Man City losing 2–0 at Stoke, we returned to top of league, and in that lofty station we stood the following week when to the King Power came Chelsea FC.

Now it may be that Mourinho was already destined to go, for the season theretofore had brought naught but misery to him, and not just in results upon the field of play, hilariously dismal though they were.

There was also the richly distasteful affair o' the comely club doctor Eva Carneiro, whom Mourinho scolded with arrogant air after to Eden Hazard's side she frantic did race, the Belgian midfielder having took one in the face.

The hazard was Mourinho's, it would transpire, since the media sided with her, and him forcefully reproved. For the rules about head injuries couldn't be clearer, and she was merely doing her job.

His grip on his own job meantime was slackening, in the fallout from that and much else. In late October, during an away match at West Ham United, he inflamed the authorities by sorely abusing the ref at half-time, compounding his already egregious offence by refusing when asked to leave the official's private sanctum, but staying to screech and to whine.

Since the referee in question was Jonathan

Moss, later to be the marshal of another Hammers game — the one at King Power (which I'll relate anon, though surely you'll not have forgot it) when he had the impudence to send Vardy off for allegedly taking a dive in the box — of his and Mourinho's encounter I say only this: a plague on both their houses.

Actually, I also say this. Beseeching your graces' pardon for the rudery, but to be pristine of mouth and a great English king need not be one and the same thing:

Who's the wa-a-anker?
Who's the wa-a-anker?
Who's the wanker in the black?
Whooo's the wa-a-a-anker in the black?

The Football Association, at Moss's suggestion, asked itself a twist on Dionne Warwick's question (as posed in a Burt Bacharach song): Do You Know the Way to Ban José? It did, as it happened, doling out a one-match stadium ban, ensuring Mourinho's absence when the Blues went to Stoke, where their crisis was deepened by another defeat. So it was that when Chelsea visited Leicester on 14 December, the Portugueser was clinging to his job, as I have said, by the flimsiest of threads.

Shortly before the clock chimed eight that

74

night, as Ranieri repaired to dugout to await the first blast of the whistle, what thoughts were flashing through his mind? Was he reflecting on previous Mourinho taunts, and dreaming of vengeance in the Italian manner of the Borgias, the Medicis and Don Corleone?

Which taunts, you ask? Such taunts as in 2004, when, embarking on his first Chelsea stint in Claudio's stead, Mourinho sneered at the poor spoken English of the man he had replaced. And such as the time in 2008, when both men were coaching in Italy, and he scornfully derided Ranieri for his failure, his age and his suppos'd complacency. 'Ranieri has the mentality of someone who doesn't need to win,' he said then. 'He is almost seventy years old . . . too old to change . . . He's old and he hasn't won anything.' (In fact Ranieri was at the time but fifty-seven, the impertinent Portuguese twat.)

Perchance, as he sat there, our Claudio was dwelling with pride on how dramatic had been the reversal of tide, how diametrical the turning of table — quite literally so, as Motty might say — with Leicester now top and Chelsea flirting with drop. 'Twas Mourinho who was now mocked as Lord of the Tossers, while Ranieri bestrode all like avuncular colossus.

That Monday, God love and protect them, Leicester were magnificent. 'We're going to win the league!' sounded across the ground, albeit tinged with an ironic gloss, though that would fade as the coming months passed. For we now were the baying hounds with scent of blood in our nostrils, and Chelsea the cornered foxes with no chance of escape.

After having mislaid them in Swansea, Vardy found his scoring boots ere long, scoring our first with a half hour gone, after he and Mahrez had linked up almost psychically, as this season they so often did. The swashbuckling Algerian, in space on the right, deftly clipped over an accurate cross, the which Jamie volleyed impeccably beyond Thibaut Courtois, the lofty Belgian betwixt Chelsea's sticks.

The second half had not long begun when Mahrez himself doubled our lead, collecting a glorious Marc Albrighton pass, sprayed fifty yards diagonally across the park, controlling the ball with a sorcerer's touch, and finding top corner from an angle acute with a swish of that wondrous left foot.

Chelsea pulled one back near the close. Too little, and too late. Three days later, on 17 December, a terse statement was duly released, which I am pleased to reproduce in full:

*Chelsea Football Club and José
Mourinho have today parted company
by mutual consent.*

Aha. In which case, I would retroactively
issue a press release regarding events that
unfolded not far from the King Power on 22
August 1485:

Statement
*Richard III and human existence have
today parted company, following the
piercing of His Majesty's midriff by a
Lancastrian sword at Bosworth Field,
by mutual consent.*

And Ranieri, what had he to say of José's
demise? 'Do you want to know the truth, the
whole truth?' he said when enquiry was
made. 'I am truly disappointed for him. When
I embraced him at the end of the match, I
was sincere.'

Now, had I declared so pious a sentiment
towards a foe whom I had lately vanquished
— expressing pity for Henry VI, perhaps, after
his death in the Tower on order of person or
persons unknown, which coincidentally set
me on the road to the throne — who would
have believed me?

Not your bard, of course. He'd have

interpret'd my words as at best verging on the tenuous, and at worst as wickedly disingenuous. Nor perchance you, my reader — or so I suspect. And mayhap nor even I. For unusually insightful as I am, I understand that the feelings within an ambitious man's breast as a struggle for power rages are neither as simple nor as pure as he would have them seem. And even when the struggle ends victoriously, the emotions, when they come, come not as single spies, but in battalions.

Yet when Ranieri spake of having only sorrow for Mourinho, 'twas almost possible to take him at face value, such a good and noble soul is he. Almost.

The truth? Aye, that I accept. The whole truth? Methinks that goes an inch too far. For surely even an angel takes a measure of delight, howe'er paltry, in the downfall of a devil that hath dissed him.

But enough now of Mourinho, whom we wave from the stage, sadly unpursued by a bear.

★ ★ ★

For each of the two Saturdays that followed, we journeyed north-westerly to take on the Scousers. Now, I love a trip to Liverpool. I go once each year on holiday, in fact, to visit my hubcaps. (Just another of my jests. No archaic, offensive stereotyping here. For whom dost thou take me? Jim 'Nick Nick' Davidson?)

And yet, Merseyside fan as I am, two games in seven days seemed to me to o'eregg the pudding. For much as we did relish our first serving of Scouse, the second turned the stomach, as you shall presently see.

First, at Goodison Park on 19 December, we bested Everton by the odd goal in five, Mahrez bolstering his tally to the tune of a brace, and Okazaki chipping in the third, the three points maintaining us at summit of the league.

With no games to be played in the coming week, we were guaranteed to spend Christmas Day on that peak, which is oft a foretelling of where a team will be come May, when the silverware they're handing out.

On Boxing Day, on the other side of Stanley Park, we took on Liverpool under their smiley new manager, the Hun Jürgen Klopp. To the delight of the Kop, we lost there 1–0.

And deservedly so, for we were curiously lethargic — like as if, being unused to the thinness of air on the mountaintop, we were stricken by altitude sickness.

So far as our tactics, we chose to sit deep, yielding possession as is ever our way, waiting to break and pierce enemy flanks, or scythe through their middle with a ball over the top. Many a battle is in such wise won, in football now as in war in my day, and the stratagem usually serves Leicester well. Yet Liverpool secured the only goal of the game, thanks to the strapping lowlander Christian Benteke. (What is it with this unseemly and novel abundance of Belgian talent? When I ruled, so far as I recall, Belgium wasn't even a country, merely a loose collection of vassal kingdoms under dominion of France and Holy Roman Empire.)

'Sooner or later we have to lose and it's OK,' said Ranieri, our own holy Roman, after the Liverpool game. 'But we only started to play when we fell behind. We were too nervous and anxious before that. I don't know why. It is important we recover now mentally.' Ye think?

Yet in our next match, at home to Man City, we once again failed to score. As did the sky blues under Manuel Pellegrini, whose tenure as boss, it was soon declared, would not outlast the season, after which he would be usurped by the much-vaunted Spaniard Josep 'Pep' Guardiola. The stars of that fixture were the two number ones, diving hither and yon to prevent any incursion of ball into net.

Much the same went for the New Year's first game, on 2 January and again at home, when Bournemouth's doughty custodian palmed away a Mahrez penalty to ensure another drowse-inducing 0–0 draw.

Four winless games in a row, three without scoring, and only three points from a possible dozen ... 'Twas our first poor run of form for many months, and our confidence plainly was dented.

So to win again soon was now wholly essential, lest a trickle of doubt about our credentials wax into a flood of proportions torrential.

Would we recover and renew the unlikeliest title challenge e'er yet seen? Or would we, like the bubbles they used forever to blow at Upton Park, and like the Chelsea reign of Jose Mourinho, fade and die?

New Year brings us to a fork in the road:
To one side — reversion to the status
    quo ante,
That tenth circle of hell forgotten e'en by
    Dante;
To the other — path to glory, a heavenly
    abode.

7

THE PRINCES AT THE POWER

*'Tis time to honour others with a pivotal
    part to play —*
*Albeit on them the spotlight does not as
    oft times shine*
*As on the genius Mahrez or on Vardy,
    peerless number nine.*
*Yet these too could be heroes — and not
    just for one day.*

The keener-witted among you will note in the preceding lines a personal homage, succinct though it be, to a minstrel of genius, great artist and sometime prancing mime.

'Tis not by mere happenstance that I sample David Bowie, though alas he was no supporter of the Foxes (or of any association football team, to the best of my knowledge. Which is considerable).

At Leicester, we are very far from o'erladen with support from popular musicians. There are the Kasabian lads, of course, and Trevor Oakes, who near half a century since did found Showaddywaddy, and did thereafter take a little walk under the moon of love. And there is the singing former prison warder Sam Bailey, a turnkey before she won *The X Factor*, shortly after which she mysteriously disappeared from public view, like those princely nephews of mine who inexplicably vanished while house guests in the Tower (a sterner prison, I'll wager, than any in which Ms Bailey e'er turn'd her key).

Truthfully, we have but a meagre spattering of fans from any of the celebrity realms. Some stake a claim to David Attenborough, who was reared close by the city with his brother, a more beloved Richard than I (though I never went around calling people 'luvvie' and sobbing at the dropping of a hat). But Sir David last attended a Foxes game, at our defunct Filbert Street fortress, more than eighty years ago. Which raises some doubt, mayhap, about the strength of his fealty to the lads.

Gok Wan, who doth gibber and prattle forth about vestments, is Leicester born and bred. But until our clappers — those archaic rattles that make such fearsome noise, which were restored unto our fans not long ago in mildly ironic tribute to days of yore — are made from silk organza rather than cardboard, a King Power regular I warrant he'll never be.

Engelbert Humperdinck spent a goodly part of his youth in the town, and by repute has a vague affection for the team. And the esteemed novelist Julian Barnes — 'Barnesy' as he be known in literary circles — is another who is Leicester born and bred, and hath a sincere passion for the Foxes to this day. As doth David Icke, who theorises so inventively, and perchance sees giant lizards lining up in the 4–4–2 formation where you and I perceive but men.

And so to Mark Selby, another local lad, who doth bend his arm to slide a wooden stick, directing multicoloured spheres hither and thither upon a table of green baize. He won the World Snooker Championship in 2014 after trailing by many frames and seeming doomed (an omen of what his club would do twelve months hence, after I in that cathedral was reinterr'd) to be crushed by Ronnie 'the Rocket' O'Sullivan.

This Selby, gaunt and pale and vampirical of aspect, goes by the sobriquet 'the Jester from Leicester'. But other than because the two words perchance to rhyme, in sooth I know not why. For he provides fewer laughs than one of Shakespeare's 'comedies', in which men confuse women with fellow men and vice versa, as if they were blind or imbecilic, or both; and which be but one third as droll as the fate that reputedly befell Edward II. (Google it for thy merriment. Unseemly would it be of me to describe it here, when for all I know you are breaking your o'ernight fast.)

Yet this Selby seems a nice boy, as Larry Grayson quoth'd, so we lend him our support each spring when to Vardy's home town of Sheffield he repairs, to chance his arm at the Crucible Theatre. And we did cheer him lustily when he paraded his trophy afore our first home game of the 2014–15 season, little thinking that within two years we would have one of our own. Speaking of which (with apologies to the Hotspurs of Tottenham and Harry Kane) . . .

He's one of our own,
He's one of our own,
Mah-ah-ark Se-e-elby,
Heeeeeeee's one of our own,
(And so's Willie Thorne!)

Other Foxes fans of distinction there must surely be, though God alone knows who. False modesty is to a sovereign anathema, so I say without apologia that the most famous Leicester fan of all — and aye, the most infamous, should a pedant you be — is me. Not a huge claim given the competition, I grant. But you can only beat what's in front of ye!

★ ★ ★

Now, the reason I adapted that line from 'Heroes' is both tragical and calendrical. After the scoreless draw with Bournemouth wherewith the previous chapter ended, our next game was on 10 January 2016. The day the musician died.

The news of Bowie's passing caused great lamentation and rending of garments to anyone who ever an adolescent misfit was; who ever felt gauche and mis-shapen and ill-fitted to this world, yet took courage from Bowie's teaching that there be no compulsion to yield to rigid orthodoxy, no need to be enshackled by the confining low expectations of others.

Leicester, who no more bend the knee to such than did he, confounding low expectations at every turn, declining to know their place, went to Tottenham that gloomsome day for the third round of the Football Association Cup. And while the title battle with Spurs was as yet unjoined, still did that game portend what was soon to come. For it was hard-fought, close, and dramatic to the last. Kane, the Harry Hotspur of the age, made it 2–2 from the spot with seconds left.

We would lose the replay 2–0, but given how sore degraded the FA Cup presently is, not a stuff nor yet a damn gave we for that. The Premier League alone obsess'd us now, and to it we did return forthwith — and not just to the Prem but to White Hart Lane, three days later, to take on the Hotspurs once again.

I cannot overstate the import of this match, for 'twas imperative to staunch the outflow of confidence, the which had seeped from us over a quartet of winless games. 'Twas paramount that the Foxes showed that inner fire, which ruthless winners like Selby, Lineker (and my good self!) above all else require.

And so we did.

'Twas not a beauteous game by highest standards, for our early-season flamboyance had by now been binned, Ranieri's focus turning to the not conceding of goals rather than the scoring in bundles thereof.

Scrappers now we were, and toe to toe with Spurs we stood throughout a hectic night. Few clear-cut chances fell to either team, but when they fell to Spurs, our Viking keeper made a longboat of himself, and ferried us to safety through the storm. Kasper Schmeichel, that godly Thor betwixt the sticks who thunders now and then at his defence when they draw his wrath — though so well do they protect the goal that seldom hath he cause to rage.

Already he had rescued us countless times, and he did so once again at White Hart Lane. An hour had passed when Kane was put through by Érik Lamela, and looked a cinch to score, until our golden Dane charged from his line, 'making himself big', in parlance of the game, and deflecting Kane's shot from his massive frame. The ball ricochet'd up onto the bar and out to safety rebounded.

We seemed headed for yet another scoreless draw — our fourth match on the bounce without a goal — when an unsung hero gave us travelling fans (and I'm there in spirit every game, kicking every ball) compelling cause to sing.

Eighty-three minutes of this frenzied game had passed when Leicester won a corner on the left. Christian Fuchs, our Austrian left back, drifted the kick beyond the Spurs back stick, to roughly midway between six-and eighteen-yard lines. And standing there, like the stately oak he is, was none other than the mighty Robert Huth.

Now, if I were obliged to tell the truth, one hand on heart the other on the Bible, the

German centre back is not one you'd think of — so far as taking a tough half-chance — as in the least reliable.

In almost three hundred top-flight games he has made the net to bulge fewer than twenty times, which makes him no match for John Terry, beside whom Huth served under Ranieri at Chelsea, before Huth's career went into decline and — like Claudio, Albrighton, and so many others — he came to Leicester City to be reborn.

That night at Hotspurs, with seven minutes left he found himself unmarked some dozen yards out. Although he had abundance of time and space, 'twas not a facile finish by any means. He stood wontedly immobile upon the spot, gravely bowed his Teuton head towards the ball, and sent it on a most exquisite arc in the opposite direction from that whence it had come.

Watched at normal speed upon YouTube, it might for slow motion be mistook, so languid did the ball leave Huth's head, so slow did it float on diagonal path, dipping late within the angle of post and bar to nestle near the top of Tottenham's net, with Spurs' Gallic keeper Hugo Lloris glancing admiringly on.

'Robert Huth, Huth, Huth!' chanted we ecstatic fans, to the tune of 'Ian Wright, Wright, Wright!' As well we might. For the ebullient Wrighty himself would have been unconscionably chuff'd to have conjured such a splendid headed goal.

Huth was a hero of epic stature that frenetic night, as have been other Foxes at other times: Fuchs and Marc Albrighton; the Dannys Drinkwater and Simpson; N'Golo Kanté, who doth dervish-like whirl in perpetual motion; later in the season when Vardy was banned (a grievous imposition to which I'll return anon), our Ghanaian whippet Jeffrey Schlupp, he too was to be a hero, albeit in his case truly just for one day.

And these our previously obscure titans were at last receiving their due credit, not merely in this land but throughout the wider world, as the feeling spread abroad that our title challenge was more than merely some transient jest.

The following week, that being said, we suffered a reverse at Aston Villa, pitiable runt of the season's litter. Mahrez missed once again from the spot — profligate Moor, must he not, like Othello, entertain the green-eyed monster when he thinks of Matt le Tissier's record from twelve yards? — when we were leading 1–0 (Okazaki). Then we let the Villans back in, settling perforce for an irksome 1–1 draw.

The next league match brought Stoke to King Power. We had them beat not long after the striking of the hour, by which we were already two ahead, subsequently adding a third for a nerve-settling 3–0 win.

'Tis the first of our scorers to whom we now turn attention, though more briefly than in justice we oughta. I refer, as that clunking set-up negates need to mention, to our midfield powerhouse Danny Drinkwater.

A box-to-box player of energy inexhaustible, the heartbeat of the team as well as its anchor, there is yet more to him than mere Duracell bunny. He proved it that day with a clinical finish after a corner was cleared beyond the edge of the area, and he scored our first of the entire league season from outside the box.

The second of our long-range strikes came hard upon the first, in the ensuing game at home against Liverpool, and that one I'll warrant you remember. For 'twas a strong Goal of the Season contender, a miraculous volley from Vardy's right boot, lashed into the net from a preposterous angle far out on the right, after he had been released by a glorious Mahrez through ball. Jamie added a second from close range soon after, to ensure a most pleasing 2–0 victory.

Premier League top four on 2 February 2016

Pos	Team	P	GD	Pts
1	Leicester City	24	18	50
2	Man City	24	23	47
3	Tottenham H	24	25	45
4	Arsenal	24	15	45

A glance at the table as it stood after that triumph sets the scene for the brace of away games to come, each at the ground of a fierce title rival, and each in its way a riveting drama — the first an uplifting history of Leicester triumphant; the second a footballing tragedy (or so did it seem at the time).

That first was at Manchester City, which is presently under the dominion of sultans of Araby, who come from the desert with limitless treasure, and buy up whate'er they please. No harm in this bit of belated rough justice. Call me prince of political correctness gone mad, but I always felt irrational guilt about what was done unto Mohammedans by my namesake Richard, whom they called 'Coeur de Lion', and others of his crusading ilk.

Be that a matter for another tome. What intrigues here is the Foxes' performance, for was there a better anywhere all season? Having torn the plutocrats to pieces like bloodlustful lions, we did feast upon their flesh like carrion crows.

Ruthless we were that afternoon — entirely, absolutely bereft of ruth. And the most unlikely scorer, here as before at Hotspurs, was Robert Huth, Huth, Huth!

The towering German guided our first in with a toe, artfully insinuating himself ahead of the unsuspecting defence to reach a Mahrez whipped cross before e'en the third minute had elapsed.

We husbanded that slender lead to the interval, for which thanks were due to Huth's defensive partner.

I speak of Wes Morgan, our unbreachable Saracen, magnificent captain, who defends the citadel wherein Schmeichel resides as if on it his very life doth depend. Here he was as so often the impervious rock on which victory rested, marshalling his troops to repel all invaders, including the Argie Sergio Agüero, who doth by and large score for fun.

Westley Nathan Morgan was born thirty-two years ago in the lace town of Nottingham, to parents who had journeyed thither from the Caribbean — and 'tis for his dam and sire's native Jamaica that he hath latterly appeared on the international stage. As with so many among our beloved Foxes, the rise to supremacy of this Captain Morgan, who commandeers and thieves the hopes of opposing strikers like a pirate of old, is undeniably rum.

He came to us from Nottingham Forest in 2010 for a paltry one million, and his worth to us now is far above rubies, this affable jewel of a man.

Now, Morgan also plies a trade beyond the field of play, as joint owner of a string of tattoo parlours wherein folk pay for images to be drawn indelibly on their skin, which may not without fierce laser beams be erased.

The name of the fourth of his establishments, which lies in Leicester's town centre, is in the style of those abundant hair salons which favour the cheesiest of puns: Ink-Credible.

Yet nothing could be more completely incredible, or more demands to be immortalis'd in ink that's indelible, than the work of this mountainous man.

Upon his own skin he has but a brace of one-word tattoos — 'Ria' and 'Roman', the names of his kids — but were I a tattoo artist, three more I'd embed thereon: 'Hero of Heroes'.

Heroic he was at Manchester City, as were all of our lads on that momentous day. After reaching half time with the fragile lead of which I have spake, we emerged from the

94

break to kill the game stone dead. Within a few minutes of the second half starting, Mahrez jinked elusively through to slam home a second. Not long after — would you it believe? — Huth scored once again, nodding home from close range when unmarked by City's unwary defenders at a set piece.

We were destroying the sky blues at will on the break, and should have scored more afore Agüero glance-headed one late, though but thin consolation to Man City that was.

Still Claudio Ranieri had only disdain when asked if he expected to sustain the title challenge to the end of the lengthy campaign, which as hath oft been observed, is a marathon and not a sprint.

'We must enjoy. This league is so strange,' the fastidious Roman told the press, wishing both to live in the moment and also to focus on the six-pointer imminently ahead. 'Now it is important to think about Arsenal.'

'So strange', forsooth, doth underplay the
    oddness of our story,
Of heroes forg'd anew from mere kooks
    and romancers.
And now to the Arsenal we went, in
    search of some new answers:
Would the boys maintain their swinging?
Would all be hunky dory?

8

LOVE'S LABOUR LOST?

O Cupid, why so cruel upon Valentine's
* Day,*
Shooting your poison arrow at our heart,
Piercing love-filled dream with venomous
* dart?*
Egregious god, couldst thou not thy foul
* hand stay?*

Perchance I, superstitious king, dwell too much upon the ominous threat of days and their numbers.

The news of Claudio Ranieri's hiring as gaffer was bruited abroad not merely in July (a month named after a Caesar who fatally ignored a warning about the danger of a date; you get my point), but on the 13th of that month, a number that strikes dread.

I reported, you will remember, that our season opener fell on the eighth day of the eighth month, and that of the number eight many — myself amongst them — are greatly afear'd, though I know not why. The bulbous shape? That eerie, circular symmetry? 'Tis odd, truly, for the number soundeth harmless enough when the bingo crier, drawing forth a coloured ball, doth jocosely yell: 'Two fat ladies — 88!'

And for Leicester indeed, these numbers of dark repute portended not ill but great good. On 8 August we o'erwhelmed Sunderland by four goals to two. As for the Ranieri announcement, suffice it that the bingo crier who introduces that thirteen with a raucous 'Lucky for some!' doth speak the purest sooth.

In this contra-intuitive spirit, mayhap it comes as no surprise that the day most treasured by romantics — and what greater romance hath any sport e'er known than ours? — should prove most hateful day of all.

For 'twas on 14 February that we progressed to London's north, to the home of Royal Arsenal. Thither we went not to pursue vengeance (the Gunners being one of but two teams to best us thus far in this season) — nay, we went to war as ardent lovers, seeking matrimony with the Premier League trophy itself.

What we found was not the stuff of sonnets, but a most brutal lesson. What we learned that chill, grey Sabbath was this: he whose death four centuries ago would be in April celebrated (and by none as joyously as I) was not the only Elizabethan poet to spew out rancid piffle.

So too did John Lyly, a contemporary of Stratford's slanderous scribe, who in his *Euphues* (of course I haven't read it; think access to a mobile library is easy wherein I dwell, do you?) wrote this:

All is fair in love and war.

Is it? Is it now?

Is it fair that in war, when but thirty-two years of age, I, Richard III, was cut down at Bosworth by some Lancastrian thug? Is it fair, do you think, that in that melancholy entertainment *Love Story*, when even younger, the pulchritudinous Ali McGraw — I pulleth a Les Dawson face, I confess, when in my mind's eye I do see her own — succumbed to a pernicious bloodly cancer?

And what befell Leicester in the final moments of the War of the Emirates . . . tell me, goodly reader, was that fair? Or was it rather a Valentine's Day massacre of the very notion of fairness?

To those who detect in the paragraphs above a rasping, cantankerous tone, I confess that too, and beg pardon of your graces. Some wounds are such gangrene to the soul that they be immune to the healing unguent of subsequent triumph. They do fester and taint all around them with their vinegar stink.

★　★　★

But before we come to this travesty of a match, as reluctantly we must, let us catch up with a listing that hath for too long been ignored.

Premier League table on 7 February 2016

Pos	Team	P	GD	Pts
2	Tottenham H	25	26	48
3	Arsenal	25	17	48
4	Man City	25	21	47
5	Man Utd	25	10	41
6	West Ham	25	9	39

Now, despite this five-point lead, remember, our title hopes were yet reckoned slender. 'Tis true, however, that the prospect had recently ceased to be deemed a mere joke. Few thought we as putative champions were having a laugh after we dismantled Man City 3–1 at their gaff. Yet still was it widely believed that ere long we would choke, as rank outsiders are wont to do.

So you will appreciate the import of this hour. Win at the Emirates, and our lead would grow to eight — sainted number in such event, never again to be afear'd! — grave harm on our enemies inflicting. A draw for us would also nicely do, taking our unbeaten run to eight (what else?), and keeping the dogs of war under Arsène Wenger — distempered Alsatian cur himself when riled, for all his professorial façade — chained within their kennel.

Yet should Arsenal win and shrink the gap to two, not only would they revive hopes which had latterly stalled; they would draw our blood. And who would be a Fox when the hounds are on the trail, closing fast upon their quarry's tail?

Lose at the Emirates, and all would think our bubble set to burst, including we ourselves. How otherwise could it be, after 132 years with no league title to our name (or rather, to our names, for as I noted many pages since, we once were Leicester Fosse).

How could we take the Premier League trophy as it shimmered in the distance as other than mischievous hallucination — like a Saharan mirage which befools a famished, thirsting man, being the manifestation of what he wouldst see rather than what is, dissolving into nothing as closer to his phantasmal goal he crawls?

With that in mind, the stage now set — to the Valentine's Day drama at the Emirates.

Lining up for us was our regular first XI, Ranieri having long laid to rest the Tinkerman ghost. I will not list all, for most you now know well, but would laud a pair who have received of attention less than their full share.

The star for us this day was N'Golo Kanté, tireless Frenchman of Malian descent, found by Steve Walsh, our eagle-eyed head scout, hidden from view at lowly Caen in Normandy — that battle-scarred French province wherein he also unearthed that priceless Mahrez jewel. Kanté signed for us in close season for a fee so modest (some £5 million) that it defieth all rhyme and reason. He is now worth tenfold that and more, however seldom he might score.

Kanté was our champion that day, making tackle after decisive tackle, breaking up attack after attack with limitless energy, launching us on the counter, generally bossing the game with the purpose, if not the malice, of an ebony Roy Keane.

Be there a better defensive midfield retriever on this planet? Gary Lineker thinks not, and did so observe on Twitter, where birds of all feathers chirrup together:

Gary Lineker

@GaryLineker

If planet Earth was ever under threat from an asteroid, I'm pretty sure that Kanté would intercept it.

Fanciful talk perhaps, but the point is truly made. Kanté did indeed intercept all the Gunners could fling at us throughout a first half in which we, thanks to him, were the stronger.

The reward was delayed till the closing minute, when Vardy won us yet another spot kick (no side in the league came close to our tally), though it was hotly disputed. For Jamie's contact with an outstretch'd leg was by some reputed to be him cunningly seeking out that limb, that over it he might plunge.

Another ref would later interpret such a collapse as deceit (see the home game versus West Ham in the following chapter, which would be so nearly an exact facsimile of this one). What, you ask, does Richard Plantagenet think? Hush now, fool — what point to canvassing me can there be? For I see such things only through spectacles tinted the Leicester blue.

Nonetheless, what is most to the purpose is that Martin Atkinson, the ref, deemed the challenge unlawful. Vardy struck the ensuing penalty to the left while the keeper plunged rightward, and raucous delight erupted in the away seats. For as football folk oft observe, with perhaps more vim and verve than so stale a thought may rightly deserve — there be no better time to score than on the stroke of half time. Meanwhile silence fell over the corporate boxes, for as the whistle shrilled for the interval, 'twas 1–0 to the Foxes.

When the second half began, it seemed to me that if the numbers on the field did equal remain — eleven of us versus eleven of them — Leicester were fated to win. For though the Arsenal appeared invigorated by whatever Wenger had said unto them at half time, my boys had developed an uncanny knack for nursing a 1–0 lead and keeping it intact, as we will learn soon enough.

Yet to answer a question posed long ago by a Dane (not Kasper Schmeichel), 'twas not to be. On fifty-five minutes, Danny Simpson, our right back, was at the soap offered first crack. Earlier booked for a trivial misdemeanour, he was now victim of a decision obscener, if anything, than that soppy first yellow card. Barely did he tug the sleeve of Olivier Giroud, a striker who stands proxy for Arsenal entire, in that he oft flatters to deceive yet little achieves, and so doth derision acquire.

The home crowd bayed and squealed to see more yellow, and Mr Atkinson, impressionable fellow, granted the mob's wish.

'Twas not Simpson's first taste of trouble, and far from the worst. The previous June he was convicted of attacking a former paramour, his child's mother, in Manchester whence he hails and where he still dwells. Penalised with a goodly load of community service, he arrived to toil at a charity shop in a Lamborghini Huracán he had purchased for two hundred grand, which some thought lacking in taste.

I make no excuses for his shameful behaviour, nor pass comment 'pon the levity of the sentence. I did bad things too (if not as bad as some make out) — and unless you deem three hundred hours of community service worse punishment than more than four hundred years of infamy at Shakespeare's hand, I paid the heavier price.

Yet 'tis e'er the supporter's way to turn blind eye to suchlike. Aye, football makes such amoral brutes of us that we would o'erlook worse — far worse — than Simpson's crime. If a certain monogonadic son of Austria (not Christian Fuchs) slipped through a tear in the fabric of space and time, as the Doctor from Gallifrey doth in his TARDIS, and won your club a trophy with a last-minute screamer from thirty-five yards, wouldst thou not in ecstasy chant, 'One Adolf Hitler, there's only one Adolf Hitler'? Methinks thou would.

But enough reflection upon football's strange power to distort the sensibilities, and back to a game in which, despite our tenacity, the balance of power had shifted decisively. Reduced to ten men, and thus bereft of our customary threat on the break, we were now wholly besieged.

A medieval warlord such as I well knows that a siege, while it may or may not frustrate the attacker, is invariably brutal on the nerves of the defence. Yet we withstood it with the fortitude of the Trojans of old under King Priam, albeit surviving unbreach'd for less than ten years. A quarter hour after Simpson's departure, on seventy minutes, came an undeserved equaliser. Theo Walcott, fleet-footed though oft witless, and on as a sub, scored from close range.

From that moment forth the Gunners unleashed all in their armoury, in wave after wave of attack Yet thanks above all to Schmeichel, to Huth and Wes Morgan, we the besieged the invaders repelled. Shredded to fragments were all of our nerve ends, yet a 1–1 draw seemed ours when the fourth official indicated a minimum of four additional minutes to play. 'Twas on that 'minimum', sad to relate, that the accent would lie.

The first of the four passed without serious incident, as did the second, and aye the third.

'Twas not until the last was up that our spirits dived to the floor of the ocean, which by now was groaning with subs.

Walcott a starring role already had played, and two others now seized the stage. Marcin Wasilewski, our Polish defender, had come on for Mahrez just before the hour, as Ranieri attempted to compensate for the deficit of a man.

With the ninety-fourth minute almost expir'd, and the ball dribbling harmlessly out for a goal kick, the venerable Pole committed an act both clumsy and needless, when a late challenge he recklessly made.

A free kick was given some thirty yards out, level with the furthest right-hand line of our box. Up stepped Mesut Özil, ethereal German of Ottoman parentage, who hath more goal assists than any other player in the kingdom. He would now add another, flighting the ball on perfect trajectory into the heart of our area as the clock ticked into the ninety-fifth minute — though time for us had long since stood still.

It fell to Danny Welbeck, on the pitch for barely ten minutes after returning from lengthy absence due to injury, to make us well sick. The ball he deflected with the faintest of headers little deviated from the path it was taking, but enough to take it inside

Schmeichel's left post.

At once time was up — and not merely for this game, but (or so it was widely believed) for Leicester's title ambitions as well.

Not since Bosworth had I felt so shitty. For a draw in such circs would have been as sweet as that triumph at Manchester City.

Gary Lineker took to Twitter once again to rail at the horror. 'Reality sucks!' read one of his declarations — and though I am unfamiliar with that vernacular, his meaning was plain. Nor was he done, for he further did ruminate upon the sport's fearful power to play havoc with the feelings, even as a fairground rollercoaster works upon the stomach, and with similarly vomitous result:

Gary Lineker
@GaryLineker
There is nothing quite like football for filling you with joy one minute and tearing your heart to shreds the next.

And so, to that, say all of us.

Now, 'tis not the way of Ranieri — no Mourinho he! — to rage at the ref in a game's aftermath. His philosophy is almost Zen-like in its *que sera sera* acceptance that what will be will be.

But not today. 'If I think about the match I

am very angry,' said a crestfallen Claudio of those soft yellow cards which were so hard on us.

Yet almost at once he recovered his *sangfroid*. 'We are still top of the table, we have two points more,' he continued. 'We lost to our opponents — we must say well done. Then we must carry on and smile.'

By the saints, I cannot count the ways in which I worship that darling man from Rome. If 'twere conceivable I would carry his babies, and I would surely have had him at my right hand when on the throne of England I sat. With him as wise, restraining Nestor to my intemperate prince, king for longer than a paltry two years I should surely have been.

His response to what our foes took to be a priceless gift — a heaven-sent boon, a decisive momentum shift — was utterly inspired. With a fortnight afore our next match, he chose to give our players, so dispirited and tired, time to lick their wounds and recover, sending them from wintry England on vacation to the sun. A mighty return on that investment would be paid, as we shall see soon enough.

O Claudio, 'twas with you I was utterly smitten
On Valentine's Day, when we were sore dejected,

Yet self-pity's lure you valiantly rejected.
I absolutely love thee. There, let that be
  written!

9

AND HAVE YOU NOW
TO BELIEVE US?

When obstacle blocked the path along
    Title Avenue,
Onus fell on us, the fans, to clear it from
    the route,
Borrowing from Mistress Delia of culi-
    nary repute:
'C'mon, best supporters in the world,
    let's be 'avin' you!'

Whatever Delia Smith contended in that memorable keynote address, when having drained her share of mead (aye, and more than her share) she urged greater noise from the Carrow Road faithful, 'tis we at the King Power who are the best supporters in the world. Fact.

Perchance the followers of all clubs would seek to appropriate that title for themselves. If so, mistaken would they be.

For 'tis us, no question. Stonewall certainty. We need no urging from bevvied-up cooks to pump up the volume at the Power. (We have no TV chef on our board, as it happens, though Rustie Lee is a big Foxes fan.)

At the KP, the volume is e'er turned up to 11. And seldom have the boys more requir'd the cacophony than when Delia's Norwich visited on 27 February, for our first game since a foolish referee unseated us from the horse (the horse, my kingd . . . ah, apologies, I did that one earlier) at the Emirates. 'Twas of the essence that we regained the saddle forthwith.

Now, though Ranieri had sent his lads on vacation to recover, scant sign was there of reinvigoration. Sluggish and out of sorts they seemed, as if the Arsenal hangover lingered. Vardy ne'er found space behind their lines, so deep and vigorous was the defence of these Canaries, parlously though they were perched on rim of relegation pit. Mahrez was off his game, jinkily dribbling once or twice, but to no gain.

All had long awaited the Leicester wobble, and here perchance it was.

It is at such a moment that any team of eleven chivalrous warriors needs the crowd to be its twelfth knight. That we were.

We lustily maintained a most rumbustious din until the end, and by the deathly shroud of Jesus, thank Christ we did, for 'twas only at the death that breakthrough came.

Propelled forth by our frantic shrieks, Mahrez released Albrighton on the right, and low he crossed at pace into the box. Vardy, sliding in, failed to connect. Ulloa, at back post, blessedly did not.

'Twould not be the only last-gasp goal the Argentine would score, and one against West Ham we will anon explore. Which mattered more I cannot say, each being supremely critical in its own way.

As Leo went to ground to be engulfed beneath his rejoicing comrades, e'en our customarily becalmed gaffer could not himself contain, Ranieri punching the air in his technical area. We in the stands surrender'd ourselves to frenzy, hugging strangers as if brothers (not as if *my* brothers, obvs; I mean as brothers with affection for their brothers).

Now, I be not fain to sexualise that goal, lest children, maidens or thy servants should perchance to read these words. Yet accretion of desire building over time, nether regions aching in urgent need of release, that juddering explosion of relief when finally it came . . .

Think not me ignorant, gentle reader, of amorous ways. I may have been rudely stamp'd, and in want of love's majesty. I may e'en, as Lady Anne did unflatteringly submit in that libellous play, have been a lump of foul deformity. Yet I e'er had a most seductive way with words. About that, if nothing else, the bard was right.

You may recall from the opening act of that travesty how I did beguile the said Lady Anne with silvery, slithery tongue, when we conversed beside her regal father-in-law's coffin. And though she believ'd 'twas I who killed him (and also her husband, if anyone be counting), and though she profess'd to wish me dead, shortly she surrender'd to my cunning lingual artistry, and later lay beside me in marriage bed.

Not to brag, but I had plenty besides (two of my three offspring were on wrong side of blanket born). For women, as has oft been remark'd, do strangely cherish an ugly man who wit and bemusing self-assurance hath. And I had both.

So doubt not, far-scattered blossom of my subjects' seed, that I comprehend the lustings of the flesh.

Yet once again it seems I do digress. So let me end these ribald musings by saying that it felt utterly orgasmic, Leo's late late winner, to this king now ectoplasmic.

'What a noise!' declared the *Match of the Day* commentator — though which I know not, since most do sound the same. All sterling fellows, no doubt, other than Jonathan Pearce, who doth for no apparent reason shout.

I esteemed the programme more highly in days of yore, when John Motson and Barry Davies ruled the roost. Motty with coat fashioned from skin of ewe and bearing notebook of a nerd, who to this day may on the highlights show be heard, albeit his value seems purely nostalgic, for his ditherings and waffle do make me neuralgic.

Davies was the guvnor, no question, for he could turn a phrase that lingers eternal. 'Look at his face! Just look at his face!' of Francis Lee. 'Samways ahead . . . and Lineker uses him by not using him!' of our own Gary (of whom more below).

'What a noise!' screamed their anonymous successor after Ulloa scored. 'And what a huge goal that could be!' Well said, sir knight, whoe'er thou may be. 'Twas verily a gigantic goal. For it hoisted us back upon that equine beast which thirteen days previous had thrown us like a bucking bronco. Small wonder, then, that in the stands we all went fucking tonto!

Three days hence, it appeared (though happily but for one day) that we had once again been unsaddled. West Brom, our visitors, took an early lead, but soon repented of their impudence with an own-goal equaliser. Making a rare midfield start that night was our longstanding valiant Andy King, and on the half hour he thrilled this randy king by putting us ahead.

We might have increased the lead, but were defied by woodwork and profligacy combined.

'Tis an iron rule of football that if chances you spurn, punished for such wastefulness you'll be. Early in the second half the Baggies levelled at 2–2 with a fine long-range free kick. Impotently thereafter did we strive for the winner.

But if the chasing pack had Foxes in their nostrils, the hounds did swiftly lose our scent. For a draw which looked a bad reverse one night was eyed anew as an advance the next, when all three of our title rivals suffered defeat.

Tottenham, who by winning would (on goal difference) have usurped us at the top, went down 1–0 at West Ham. Man City were trounced 3–0 by Liverpool at Anfield. As for Arsenal . . . 'Tis height of poor form to make sport of another's mishap, I own it. But losing at home to Swansea after scoring first? Arsenal had wholly blown it, and how in sooth not to snigger at that?

That triplefold failure firmed up the suspicion that the title and Leicester — surely the unlikeliest partners to be joined in wedlock since Elton John and that German bint — was a marriage meant to be.

Our quartet of ensuing fixtures cemented

the conviction, and may be succinctly related by thieving a chant from the Arsenal era of George Graham, who did enjoy a bung:

One-nil to the Le-e-eicester!

* * *

In none of these encounters were we anywhere approaching our best, for they were scrappy performances and unlovely to the eye. But 'tis the mark of champions, or so I have heard tell, that they find a way to win when not playing well.

First to Watford, erstwhile dominion of that outlandish groom Sir Elton, whereat Mahrez scored the solitary goal requir'd not long before the hour. We then hosted lowly Newcastle, the lone strike coming from Okazaki, who scored with an o'erhead kick as if back in the Orient a circus performer he had been.

Next to Crystal Palace, where Mahrez again notched all we needed, profiting from role reversal to turn in a Vardy cross. After a scare in added time when Palace struck our crossbar, we fans were so o'erjoyed to have prevail'd that we ignored many requests over the Tannoy to take our leave of Selhurst Park, remaining behind and relentlessly singing:

We're gonna win the league,
We're gonna win the league.
And now you better belieeeee-eve us,
We're gonna win the league!

Next Southampton ventured to our strong-hold to try their luck, and found none. They had the lion's share of possession, as teams opposing us so oft do. But our winner came before half time against the run of play, and few of all our goals gave us such pride as this. For 'twas Wes Morgan, noble leader of men, who headed home a cross from Christian Fuchs.

O captain, my captain!

Five 1–0s from six games drew close to six from seven, when next north to struggling Sunderland we journeyed. Having failed to bulge a net since Valentine's Day, Vardy was enduring a goal drought, in parlance of the game.

It never raineth but it poureth! Here he bagged a second-half brace: the first a wont-edly laconic finish when released by astute Albrighton; in added time he did round the keeper for a facile second.

Tottenham appeared our only true rivals for the title now, and after they that day smote Man Utd 3–0, the table was as you see below:

Premier League top six on 10 April 2016

Pos	Team	P	GD	Pts
1	Leicester City	33	26	72
2	Tottenham H	33	35	65
3	Arsenal	33	22	59
4	Man City	33	25	57
5	Man Utd	33	9	53
6	West Ham	33	12	52

Those same turf accountants who in August had us for champions at 5,000–1, now in April adjudged us odds-on at 1–4, which doth virtually equate to a dead cert.

Yet April be the cruellest month, as a poet once writ (not him; can't always be him — 'twas T.S. Eliot) — and bearing that in mind, even now I did not dare to tempt fate, lest it transform the verdant paradise visible ahead into a waste land of dreams denied.

Who knows better than I, Richard, last of England's kings in battle to die, that in war calamity may at any moment be plucked from triumph's slack jaw?

And thus it very nearly came to pass in our next game.

The visitors on 17 April were the in-form

cockney swaggerers of West Ham, recent conquerors of the Hotspurs and challengers themselves for a Champions League berth. 'Twas never going to be easy. We foresaw that we would have to play for all we were worth — but not that the referee would be as absurd as any on whom we e'er clapped eyes.

For nigh unto an hour, all went exceeding well. Vardy scored early after being released by Kanté, and given our recent happy record with a 1–0 lead we fans felt at our ease.

Ten minutes into the second half, all changed. Vardy sped into the West Ham box, and there collapsed as if felled by an arrow. When whistle blew, the joyous King Power as one thought this: Penalty!

But then the realisation spread slowly, like hemlock through the veins paralysing a body limb by limb, that Jonathan Moss had given it the other way, perceiving that Vardy the contact had manipulated in order to feign a deliberate trip where none in fact had been. Worse yet, he showed the number nine a yellow card. Worst of all, 'twas Jamie's second of the game, he having received one for little cause in the first period.

Exit Vardy, pursued by barefaced cheek of a ref who would report him to the justices of the FA for jabbing an accusatory finger, thereby having his automatic one-match ban redoubled to two. Infamy!

As Jamie departed, anguishing remembrance flooded back. At the Emirates, 'twas at the identical point of the game, some five minutes before the hour, that Danny Simpson had repaired to dressing room for an early shower, after a second yellow when his first had been every squidgy inch as soft as Jamie Vardy's.

What ensued on Valentine's Day I outlined in bowel-wrenching detail in the preceding chapter. But for any who suffers amnesia, our 1–0 lead was flipped, after down to ten we went, to a 2–1 defeat. How hateful close upon a perfect replica of that we came this day.

Karl Marx it was who said that history repeateth itself, first as tragedy, the second time as farce. So it proved here, the outcome being more comic than the tragic one against the Arse.

Yet mirth was in scant supply as we heroically mounted the rearguard, stoically repelling the Hammers' potent attack until, six minutes from full time, victory was in plain sight. Then a seemingly harmless cross was cleared out of our box, and obscure the reason was to us when Moss pointed to the spot. The replays, to be fair, revealed that Wes Morgan had had his hands around one of his foes — yet if a penalty be given for all such as that, a cricket score would in every game amass.

When the brawny Andy Carroll, on as sub, duly found the net, 'twas no longer a matter of winning but of clinging to one point. Two minutes later, e'en that paltry ambition receded. A Hammers cross reached their left back Aaron Cresswell, who struck it on the volley as if firing a bolt from crossbow, far beyond Schmeichel's flailing dive.

We were winded as if punched in solar plexus, trapped in that unholy nexus where fanciful dreams meet the reality which, so Lineker tweeted, 'sucks'.

And yet, and yet . . . deep in added time, taking a pass from Christian Fuchs, Jeffrey Schlupp of sizzling pace, who earlier had Marc Albrighton replaced, assailed the left of West Ham's box. Andy Carroll, doing God knows what back there, connected shoulder-wise with the substitute Fox.

Down went Schlupp. Up went Moss's hand, gesturing at the white chalk spot twelve yards from goal. A scant seven seconds of added time remained when that penalty was awarded.

With neither Vardy nor Mahrez on the pitch, it fell to Leo Ulloa to step up.

I wouldst not at that hour have been the

Argentine — not for all the realms of France and Spain. For can your fancy conceive the pressure on his head, knowing the excruciating pain in wait should he miss?

He did not. Belying the crushing pressure, he calmly strode forth and struck the ball cleanly into the right of West Ham's net.

Lineker took to Twitter, his verdict to deliver.

Gary Lineker
@GaryLineker
I don't think that's a penalty, to be honest but sod it! Great point.
3:22 PM — 17 Apr 2016

Sod it indeed. For after the earlier spot-kick rank injustice which robbed us of victory, whether ours was more merit'd, who gave a tinker's toss? The contest had been rendered farce by Mr Moss. Yet while we laughed from relief more than the refereeing slapstick, the Hotspurs knew that in dropping those two points we had missed a trick.

Next night those crowing cockerels went to Stoke and played them off the pitch, winning 4–0 when it might have been six, narrowing our lead to five points with four matches to play. They had the momentum, 'twas widely acknowledg'd, and the Foxes — Vardyless now, for woe, for woe! — might yet be prey of chickens.

The winds of fortune were redirected
    once again,
By one who in error pointed to the spot.
    Cur!
To billow the sails of resurgent Totten-
    ham Hotspur.
Was the title heading now to White Hart
    Lane?

10

AND SO IT ENDS

Four to play, and all might still go wrong,
For landmines in the Foxes' path yet lie.
Claudio, do thou issue thy battle cry:
'Dilly-ding, my sons. And dilly-dong!'

Funny old game, the pep talk.

How best for a general to stir sinews and gird loins? How to focus minds that may be wandering under pulverising stress? How to extract the very best from your lads?

Some coax, some cajole. One seeks to motivate with fear, another beseeches heightened effort with blandishing words.

I, Richard, addressing troops on eve of battle, was more a stick than carrot guy. All blood and thunder, I saved my wooing, cooing words for the girls (of whom, as I may have mentioned, I had my portion, withered runt or not).

And if any man should let me down, quite the Sir Alex Ferguson was I. I would stand close by he who offended me — on a soapbox if needed, for many were a foot taller than I and more — spewing such fiery words upon

124

his head that afore long his hair, though newly rinsed, was dry.

Claudio Ranieri is cut from different cloth. He does not screech or bully. He does not give vent to wrath, nor kick out in ire at a discarded boot, that it fly up and slash eyebrow upon the girlish visage of David Beckham (who doth crave such plethora of inked images upon his form, he might keep Wes Morgan's tattoo parlours in profit until Judgement Day and beyond).

No, Ranieri speaks to his boys as a caring father speaks to his when to manhood's estate they have come. With concern and respect, firm when requir'd, aye, but never harsh nor rasping, much less cruel.

Now, Shakespeare inked me indelibly in his verbal painting — which doth make Dorian Gray's portrait look like *The Mona Lisa* — as a pathological teller of lies.

At times, perforce I fibbed, as men do when playing deathly game of thrones. Yet about this it is pointless to lie: oft times I did weep in the season newly past.

Strong men cry, as the big Lebowski says in the filmic entertainment that bears his name, and so it is. When Vardy broke that scoring record, my tears flowed beyond containment. When Danny Welbeck glanced home Arsenal's winner on Valentine's Day, they flowed again for woe rather than joy.

And yet nothing sent my lachrymals so wild, with the tears issuing forth not in a trickle but an oceanic tide, as when Claudio spoke of his feelings for his side.

Not long afore the PFA annual dinner on 24 April, whereat was revealed who all the league's players had chosen as their champion, half the six nominated being Vardy, Kanté and Mahrez, Ranieri said this: 'I am very proud because they deserve it. They are doing a fantastic performance in every match and I hope one of them can win. They are three sons for me. If one son wins I am very happy.'

And yet more upon the theme had he to say: 'But all my players should be on the list. They are all my sons, they are sons for me and I would like all my sons there.' Lyrical, is it not, how he phrases the thought? And unbearably moving to envisage him, loving sire of such a brood, swelling with fatherly pride.

Now, loath I be to praise a certain bard, yet every now and then that scrofulous scribe doth hit a nail upon the head. Well, even a broken clock showeth the right time twice a day. In *The Merchant of Venice*, he has Launcelot say, ''Tis a wise father who knows his child.'

'Tis truth that few fathers comprehend their issue, knowing how they tick and how to keep them ticking, so that they be ne'er like a stopped clock, but are true at all times of the day.

Claudio is such a father to his sons, valuing their strengths and knowing how to increase them, comprehending their weaknesses and how they may be abated, finding ideal words to lift them when their confidence hath cratered.

And if their concentration be lapsing and their focus drifting — to women, gaming, or motoring machines of the sort 'neath which I lay in that noxious car park — what stirring oratory does Ranieri conjure to set them right on battle's eve? I shall tell ye.

Dilly-ding, dilly-dong!

'Tis hardly that Lancastrian toerag Henry V at Agincourt, now is it?

The liege lord that dilly-ding, dilly-dong suggests to me is another — an actor who as a Grace Brothers character did serve on menswear counter.

For in truth, Claudio doth closely resemble the late John Inman. (Watch any episode of *Are You Being Served?* if to doubt me you have the insolence.)

And Inman's Mr Humphries, when asked if he be at liberty, by Captain Peacock or Mrs

Slocombe who was fore'er repairing home to stroke her pussy, would reply in falsetto squeal, 'I'm freeeeeeeeee!'

Like him, Ranieri now hath a catchphrase of his own.

Dilly-ding, dilly-dong.

'Twas revealed in interview by Danny Drinkwater, the midfield stalwart who can by no foe be intimidated (you can lead a force 'gainst Drinkwater, but you cannot make him blink!).

And Ranieri did himself confirm it: 'From the beginning when something was wrong, I've been saying, 'Dilly-ding, dilly-dong, wake up, wake up!' So on Christmas Day I bought for all the players and all the staff a little bell. It was just a joke.'

I am hardly one to brook bell-related merriment, for such cannot help but bring to mind Quasimodo. And no hunchback can be seemly source of mirth.

Yet 'dilly-ding, dilly-dong' casts a grin across my face, like so many quips which Claudio hath made. For always is he good in fooling, and hath such an amusing way with words.

Here is a smattering of Ranieri's jestings, that we might find refreshment in levity afore I describe the seasonal dénouement with wonted brevity:

Selection of droll Ranieri quotes

'Why can't we continue to run, run, run? We are like Forrest Gump. Leicester is Forrest Gump.'

'I don't believe in the bookmakers. The bookmakers at the beginning predicted the first manager sacked would be Ranieri. The first!'

'I said to the players, 'When we keep a clean sheet, I pay for everyone a pizza.' Maybe they wait for me to say, 'OK, a good dinner instead.' They seem to be waiting until I improve the offer. Maybe a pizza and a hot dog!'

'I told my players, 'When you go on the pitch and you hear the song from Kasabian, that means they want warriors.' I want to see them as warriors for the fans. Kasabian are a fantastic rock band from Leicester and I think the guitar man, Serge, is Italian.'

'I am waiting for the whole stadium to sing 'Dilly-ding, dilly-dong'.'

Mayhap the KP faithful will oblige afore too long.

Ranieri is truly the Jester from Leicester, and not the saturnine Mark Selby, though the latter did heap our happiness pyre yet higher by reaching once again the world snooker final, in Sheffield whence Jamie Vardy came.

In this time of miracles, it seemed less coincidental than entirely inevitable that Selby would be there. For on the afternoon of Sunday, 1 May, the snooker final began at the exact moment Leicester kicked off against Man Utd in the match that would, if won, the title secure.

Selby is a righteous Foxes fan, and lest his mind might drift to Old Trafford from the green baize, lest he needed to refocus with a catchy little phrase, his opponent in that final was (Dilly-) Ding.

Aye, 'twas Ding Junhui from distant China whom Selby played. And 'twas on the following night, as Spurs were at Stamford Bridge for another potential title decider, that the snooker final bubbled to its climax.

And when the Chinese wondered for whom the bell tolled, Selby answered (not at all in jest): 'Dilly-Ding Junhui, it tolls for thee!'

'Tis at this point one heareth not the chiming of a bell, but the do-do-doooo-do do-do-doooo-do of the *Twilight Zone* theme tune. Couldst thou make up such alignment of the stars in Leicester's favour? Methinks not.

Yet we are premature. Before that Man Utd fixture and Tottenham's disorderly game at Stamford Bridge, let us return to previous matches involving these two rivals.

When we left matters after our farcical draw with West Ham, the table stood as below. With Arsenal and Man City by the wayside fallen, I restrict the featured teams to the relevant twain.

Premier League top two on 18 April 2016

Pos	Team	P	GD	Pts
1	Leicester City	35	30	76
2	Tottenham H	35	39	69

The experts suspected the two teams' respective thirty-fifth games of the season might set in motion the awaited Leicester implosion: that if we, toothless for want of suspended Vardy, failed at home to defeat Swansea, and if Spurs then o'ercame West Brom the next night, narrowing the points gap to two or three, then . . .

But no, e'en now I cannot take that phantom fear and give it corporeal being upon the page.

So much, my lords and ladies, for the experts. They had discounted us time and time and time again. Not that I really blame them. Who berates a man for being sceptical about the wholly unbelievable? Yet how wide of the mark those pundits were now was barely conceivable. Knew they nothing still about how firm and straight our spine? (And no jesting, thanking you, about mine.)

A few hours before that PFA dinner, our nerves were swiftly settled against Swansea at the Power. Vardy was replaced by Leo Ulloa, and a splendid stand-in he would prove after Mahrez led the way.

Nine minutes had passed when a defender, misclearing a ball from edge of his own box, found our glorious Moor. He sauntered through, swaying one way, then the other, before calmly striking home. 'Twould be a signal day for the Merlin of Maghreb, as will become apparent anon.

As the half hour was set to chime . . . dilly-ding, dilly-dong, again it's goal-scoring time!

Danny Drinkwater whipped in a cross from the left, which Ulloa coolly headed inside the post.

This game was as good as done. Two more were added after the break, the first another for Leo, the second from Marc Albrighton, and so did it conclude 4–0.

Albrighton had been dropped for this game, not for want of form but lack of speed, for with Vardy absent we were sorely shorn of pace. To compensate, Claudio selected in his stead on the left the greyhound Jeffrey Schlupp, who rewarded the boss's faith by having a blinder.

Now, many would know the secret of Leicester's success. 'Tis a mystery not resolved in facile manner, for a myriad of factors must have coalesced. Yet one on which I would reflect is the lack of ego shown by the lads. Whene'er one of them was dropped for strategic gain, as Albrighton for the Swansea game, no shred of rancour did he show. No queenly tantrum did e'er one throw.

Ulloa, star of previous season's great escape, this one did accept his supersub role, sitting placid on the bench awaiting any chance to serve. He knew perchance that which evaded me long ago: that not all men to king's estate should come, and at times 'tis better if another wears the crown.

Another revealing moment came late in this game, when the boss sent Albrighton on for tiring Schlupp. Marc fondly hugged the man who in the starting XI did him replace, the two sharing a joke along with the embrace.

This told a lesson which others might learn about the lack of that narcissism and internecine rivalry which in many a more vaunted dressing room causes tension, destroying all-important unity at some clubs one might mention.

Before Spurs could respond the following night, Claudio and his sons, time being tight, flew to London for that PFA dinner, in a fleet of those whirling metal birds which, as I have noted ere now, deposit our Thai chairman on KP turf before each game, and after the final whistle take him off again.

There was Riyad Mahrez anointed Footballer of the Year.

Who would gainsay that? While none of Ranieri's sons had been other than magnificent, Mahrez was a most deserving recipient. For not only did he score almost as many as Jamie, and assist more often than almost any other. He had the uncanny gift, this Moorish alchemist, which transforms a strong but slightly leaden side into gold — the ability to do that which none foresees, talent to surprise which few possess. Eric Cantona had it at Leeds and Man Utd, as did Glenn Hoddle and poor, dear Gazza, both for Hotspurs.

His gift for bamboozlement made him more than PFA Player of the Year. In mine eyes it makes him Leicester City's Player of All Time.

And who but I am qualified to say? For who else has seen every single Foxes game — aye, and kicked every ball they ever kicked — since we were founded as Leicester Fosse in 1884, one year shy of four centuries after I at Bosworth fell?

Even among our manifold renaissance tales — Vardy reborn as an international; Albrighton dishonoured by Aston Villa before his revival; Wes Morgan, undercard player turned headliner; Ranieri, sacked by the Hellenes after two Faroe Islands defeats, risen phoenixlike from his Grecian urn . . .

Of all these resurrections, none (other perhaps, saving your graces, than my own, and its transformative effect) is more remarkable.

Born twenty-five years ago in a Parisian suburb peopled by many from North Africa whence his parents came, one from Morocco, the other Algerian, at but fifteen young Riyad suffered the death of his father.

'Twas a pulverising blow, for his father was also his mentor in football and all things, and thenceforth did the boy dedicate himself to honouring the sire who expired. To this day, he says that all he doth, he doth for he who passed.

No one disputed his precocious talent, only his physique, for too flimsy was he deemed for the highest league. Once he came close to signing for St Mirren in Scotland, from which barbarous land, when I fought battles, I could not wait to flee south.

Mahrez felt so too. He could not withstand the Caledonian weather, which is indeed vile, and so left his kit behind during his St Mirren trial, borrowing a bicycle to pedal away as fast as he could.

He went instead to the French port of Le Havre, where Steve Walsh, our lord of recruitment, saw beyond a slender frame which weighs not ten stone.

Look at him now, that reedy, skinny lad. See what he does for the father who died and for his Italian second dad, he whom all others thought too slight, lacking Steve Walsh's insight.

Sorrows, as I have remarked, come not as single spies but in battalions, aye — yet now and again 'tis the same way with pleasures. The night after Mahrez's PFA coronation, delight upon delight for Foxes all, when Tottenham suffered a devastating fall.

Their crowing caught in the Hotspur cockerels' throats when 1–1 they were held at home by West Brom. Transcendent joy for us; cataclysm for them.

In Ranieri style, I'll tell ye a joke
Of pundits who until the last anticipated
That to buckle 'neath stress were we fated.
And in the end 'twas Tottenham who
*   did choke!*

With three games to play, another glance at the league table is due, and pleasing to the eye will it be.

Afore that, however, some sympathetic words for a few Leicester fans. You may disbelieve that such be requir'd for any so richly blest. Let me tell you of such pitiable folk nonetheless.

First, Gary Lineker, Leicester born and bred, season-ticket holder since boyhood, who as a child cried all the way home after our 1969 FA Cup ~~semi~~-final defeat to Man City. He who now, when not vending fried crisps of potato on behalf of Walker's, the name of which firm adorned our stadium before Siamese merchants came and King Power renamed it, doth moonlight as genial host of *Match of the Day*.

Gary is a noble man by nature, and one day surely a nobleman will be by rank. Were I king yet, I would create him Earl, if not Duke, of Leicestershire, in reward for his efforts of yore as our goal-hanging gallant. What her present Majesty imagines she is doing by not so much as touching his shoulder with her sword, I know not.

Now, never in his long career did Gary receive a yellow card, that much I do know. Perchance the colour be a phobia, for he himself hath not the vestige of a yellow streak.

With courage far beyond the call of duty, as

neared its end the year 2015, yond Lineker did tweet the binding oath that if the title was won, he would present the show clad only in his kecks.

> **Gary Lineker**
> *@GaryLineker*
> *YES! If Leicester win the @premierleague I'll do the first MOTD of next season in just my undies.*
> *9:54 PM — 14 Dec 2015*

Sympathies to him, for he will be grievous ribbed by such as Mark Lawrenson, who for reasons beyond fathoming fancieth himself a wit. 'Banter' his comedy stylings be called, though ne'er need anyone hearing him shriek out, 'Good nurse, Lawro's cracked another! Come quick! Hasten to my aid with the ribcage repair kit!'

Pity those also who, having backed us in August, lacked the bottle to stick to their guns, and cashed out betting slips before the race was run. Fellows like an unnamed man of Warwickshire who, so reported the *Sun*, wagered £50 at 5,000–1, but settled with Ladbrokes for £72,335.

While I have no time for denizens of that West Midlands region, which calls itself 'Shakespeare's County' upon motorway sign,

I yet understand this lily-livered act, since almost all presumed that we would fade ere spring had sprung.

Lastly, a consoling thought for me, of whom God willing you think better than afore you read this dissertation, yet who fears the stigma of the centuries will cling to his reputation.

'Tis ill enough to be immortalis'd as wickedest of kings in Shakespeare's words, yet to live eternally in East End rhyming slang is worse. To this day, a cockney fellow espying canine befoulment upon the way will caution his friend, 'Watch yerself, me old china, or you'll put a foot in that Richard the Third!' 'Twould be pleasing if another king could substitute for me, even as Leo Ulloa doth oft relieve Okazaki.

So do this small favour for me if in any way you have relished my book. If ever thou perceive a dog mess on the street, and would warn another to take heed, say this in your best Ray Winstone tones: 'Take care, me old mucker, lest you step in that Edward the Third.'

Yet rile me though it doth to be butt of such vulgarity, I find myself in these times more given to hilarity than for many hundred years. For Leicester's epiphany has effected a change upon my humour like that wrought on the miser Scrooge by the spirits which did visit him early doors on Christmas Day.

And now back to the lethally serious business at hand, and the table peak as promised above.

Premier League top two on 18 April 2016

Pos	Team	P	GD	Pts
1	Leicester City	35	30	76
2	Tottenham H	35	39	69

Now, I'm no Carol Vorderman who doth perform such rapid arithmetical calculations, much less a Stephen Hawking who penetrates the ancient mysteries of the cosmos.

For all that, one need have but little mastery of sums to unravel this conundrum. All requir'd now for Leicester to clinch the title was three points, assuming Tottenham won their remaining games.

Whate'er those Hotspurs might do, one more win was now all that stood between us and promised land. In quest of that outlandish fantasy, we progressed — where else? — to what for once might justly be called the 'Theatre of Dreams'. To Old Trafford on 1 May went we, Vardy-less, and there endured a hideous start. We were behind within ten minutes to a goal from the aptly named Anthony

Martial, bellicose striker that he is, despite his tender years.

United would have scored more but for our Viking custodian. Watched by Peter Schmeichel, his Old Trafford legend of a sire, Kasper did both him and his second dad Claudio proud.

We were in deep bother all the same, tormented on the right flank where our full back could scarce be found, for Danny Simpson was having a 'mare. And in no wise was it a horse for which anyone on speaking terms with sanity their kingdom would have traded.

On May Day, when the distress call went out, who to the rescue came? Who but our captain in the field, our Saracen Wes Morgan, finding space in the United box to head the equaliser when but seventeen minutes had elapsed.

Our nerve recovered, we never relapsed, and might have won the title there and then. For in the second half when all was square still at 1–1, we uncloaked the flamboyance that had been hidden for so long. Our counter-attacks, replete with artful, telling flicks, came close to undoing de Gea on guard betwixt United's sticks.

'Twas not to be, and after Danny Drinkwater saw red late on for a tug on the very perimeter of the box — the myopic ref, bless him, judged it outside — we were content to leave with a point. For it meant that unless Hotspurs won next night against Chelsea at Stamford Bridge (no happy hunting ground for them), the title would be ours.

The title would be ours . . . how remarkable even now to think that so monumental a notion may into six short syllables be condensed!

All envisaged before the season's start
Chelsea at centre stage when it ended.
And so they were, though not as they
    intended,
For here we find them in supporting part.

'Twould be a most vital supporting part for all that.

But how did Ranieri plan to watch the game that might bestow upon him his first managerial title?

At Stamford Bridge itself? If not there, at the home of Jamie Vardy (that day anointed the Football Writers' Player of the Year), where his honorary sons would foregather in hope of seeing this war concluded as they had fought all its battles: as a few, a happy few, a band of brothers.

None of the above. Ranieri would not watch the game at all, so it was reported. On the Sunday after the Man Utd game he flew to Rome, eternal city of his birth, to see his Italian mama, and next day take her out for lunch to celebrate her ninety-sixth birthday.

His flight home on the Monday, in our chairman's Gulfstream private jet, would span the Tottenham game entirely. He would be last alive to know the score. Or so the tabloids would have had us believe. Common sense suggests that could not be. For would not the pilot beg tidings from air-traffic control, and issue announcements to keep our boss in touch? Such as: 'This is the captain speaking. We are climbing to an altitude of 36,000 feet, and anticipate a little turbulence, so wouldst thou kindly fasten thy safety belts? And should the gentleman in seat B4 who doth resemble John Inman be interested, 'tis my distasteful duty to relay news from the control tower at Rome airport that Harry Kane hath given the Hotspurs a thirty-fifth-minute lead at the Bridge.'

Before the whistle blew to conclude the first half of a spiteful, fractious encounter, Spurs had doubled their lead. It seemed then certain that the race would endure; that we must wait for Everton on Saturday the title to secure.

Any subsequent captain's bulletin would have brought more heartening news. For shortly before the hour their arrears were halved by Blues.

And how, you may wonder, did I, Richard III, cope as the building of tension became unsupportably great? In the hope that a distraction would allow the fever to break, I turned to the snooker on BBC2, where Leicester fan and local hero Mark Selby was suffering at hands of Ding Junhui, who took three frames in a row on comeback trail even while Spurs were scoring twice.

Yet soon after Chelsea pulled that goal back, Selby returned the Chinese to his torturer's rack, winning the next to put himself a mere one frame short of winning his title, just as we were a goal shy of ours. The symbiosis was uncanny. Nor was it done quite yet.

With the clock running down at Stamford Bridge, Chelsea were in the ascendant. It felt to me as if some internal dynamic was driving this game to a melodramatic ending. It was.

Now, many late goals have been detailed in pages previous — the Welbeck strike which broke the heart on Valentine's Day; Ulloa's against Norwich which repaired and made it soar. But of all the last-gasp goals that peppered this campaign, none was more needed than one we neither scored nor conceded.

Seven minutes remained at Stamford Bridge when Chelsea advanced along the

Hotspurs' left flank. Eden Hazard is the Belgian to whose cranial injury the Chelsea doctor Eva Carneiro famously attended early in the season, to the snarling rage of that unmannered dog Mourinho.

This time, 'twas Tottenham's head he would do in, collecting the ball just inside their box, curling it on an exquisite trajectory, so that it bent an inch within the post, and dipped another beneath the bar. The game was tied at 2–2, and if so it stayed for some few minutes more . . .

It did. Cherished reader, it did!

Those minutes, which with added time numbered a quarter hour, passed with bare a threat to Chelsea's goal. For Spurs did what to Ranieri would be unthinkable, and in their desperation gave away their dignity, kicking and hissing and snapping and snarling, and sacrificing the chance to grab the winner on the altar of searing disappointment.

From Jamie Vardy's party with his con-freres, our Viennese lion Christian Fuchs did kindly post 'pon social media video footage of the delirium when final whistle blew.

Of Ranieri, meantimes, there was still no sign. And yet invisible as he was, I saw him in my mind's eye clear, smiling the beatific smile of the saint he is, wiping away a blissful tear as he reflected on what he and his sons had done, they who nine month ere were 5,000–1.

Me? I switched back to BBC2 to check on our town's other jester, and there thirteen minutes after that Bridge war was over, Mark Selby did beat Junhui, by eighteen frames to fourteen.

Dilly-Ding had been dilly-donged by Leicester, as had Tottenham, Arsenal, Man City and the rest of 'em. Selby stood upon the Crucible stage, and did what any Foxes fan would have him do, enshrouding himself in the club banner under which we all march.

★ ★ ★

For myself, I stayed awhile within my tomb, dwelling on all that had occurr'd these fourteen months, from last March's imminent doom to the triumph of this night. I thought of Nigel Pearson, who led us clear of relegation peril when least expected, and sitteth within the pantheon for that.

I thought of the prayers that were answered — and not just by He who presides over Christian souls in this cathedral, but by whoever heard the words of the Buddhist monks who before each game chanted imprecations on the urging of our owners from Siam.

I thought of those who are the backbone of

our club — players, coaches and scouts, of course, but also groundsmen and medics, tea ladies, cleaners and office staff too. And I thought of we who, whatever Delia professes, are by far the greatest supporters the world has ever seen.

Only then did I leave my sanctified resting place, floating off upon a cloud of exhilaration, singing to myself Leicester songs which scarce befit my kingly station, as I flitted from cathedral to the ground, a journey of a little less than a mile, whither those fans had congregated in their thousands.

And there at the King Power I bathed in the ineffable bliss I knew for not a moment in life, for hour after hour after hour.

> Be it your graces' pleasure, 'tis time to
>   leave
> This tale of how since I, King Richard
>   III,
> Was from car park releas'd, and reinterr'd,
> Of glory we dared dream, perchance
>   believe.
> Heroes there are, and far too many to
>   name,
> Who played their part in bringing into
>   being
> That which mystifies the eyes for all the
>   seeing:

Foxes fossilised in amber of eternal fame.
What role in it was played by this old
   king?
'Tis where my book began, and where it
   endeth,
That question of what my reburial por-
   tendeth
Of the miracle which across the world
   did ring.
The battle cry that drove us to the zenith:
'Dilly-ding, dilly-dong!' A chime to best
   all chimes,
A clarion call for these and any times.
That's all from me, I've now had my
   twopenn'orth.

So I have, but others have one last thing to add which may cast light upon the grand question hinted at throughout this tome.

'Tis to my fellow fans at the KP that I leave the final words. They sang this song at every game, home and away, to the tune of 'Those Were the Days', a ballad recorded to vinyl by various down the years, most famously by Mary Hopkin:

Leicester City chant about the author
Those were the days, my friend,
We thought they'd never end.
We found a king in the town car park.

And now with king power,
The Premiership is ours.
We are Leicester City FC.

We do hope that you have enjoyed reading this large print book.

Did you know that all of our titles are available for purchase?

We publish a wide range of high quality large print books including:
Romances, Mysteries, Classics
General Fiction
Non Fiction and Westerns

Special interest titles available in large print are:
The Little Oxford Dictionary
Music Book
Song Book
Hymn Book
Service Book

Also available from us courtesy of Oxford University Press:
Young Readers' Dictionary
(large print edition)
Young Readers' Thesaurus
(large print edition)

For further information or a free brochure, please contact us at:
Ulverscroft Large Print Books Ltd.,
The Green, Bradgate Road, Anstey,
Leicester, LE7 7FU, England.
Tel: **(00 44) 0116 236 4325**
Fax: **(00 44) 0116 234 0205**

Other titles published by Ulverscroft:

ANOTHER MOTHER'S SON

Janet Davey

Lorna Parry is the mother of three sons: Ewan, who hides himself away in his bedroom; Oliver, away for his first year of university; and Ross, in the lower sixth, who is giving his teachers 'cause for concern'. In the claustrophobic loneliness of her own home, she orbits her children and struggles to talk to them — still angry at her ex-husband, uncomfortable around her father's new girlfriend, and working quietly as the last remaining employee in a deserted London archive. Life seems precariously balanced. Then a shocking event occurs in the stationery cupboard at Ross's school, and Lorna's world threatens to implode . . .

PRECOCIOUS

Joanna Barnard

They say your school days are the best of your life. But everybody lies . . . Fiona is (un)happily married when a chance meeting with her former teacher Mr. Morgan plunges her headlong into an affair. But as their obsessive relationship grows ever darker, Fiona is forced to confront her own past. She first drew close to Henry Morgan as a precocious and lonely fourteen-year-old, and their relationship was always one which she controlled — or did she? Are some of the biggest lies Fiona has told been to herself? Has Henry Morgan been the love of her life, or the ruin of it?